Table of Content

Chapter-1	Innovation: Introduction
Chapter-2	Innovation Management
Chapter-3	Innovation Management as a source of Competitive Advantage
Chapter-4	Dynamic Capability
Chapter-5	The evolution of the dynamic capabilities concept

- 5.1 The Resource-Based View
- 5.2 Organisational Routines View
- 5.3 Organisational Capabilities View
- 5.4 Dynamic Capabilities View

Chapter-6 Classification of Dynamic Capabilities

- 6.1 Marketing Capability
- 6.2 Human-Resource Retention Capability
- 6.3 Right Sizing capability
- 6.4 Investment Capability
- 6.5 Production Capability
- 6.6 Absorptive capacity
- 6.7 Leadership Capability
- 6.8 Collaboration Capability

Chapter-7	Innovation Management Capability
Chapter-8	Summary
BIBLIOGRAPHY	

Chapter 1:

Innovation: Introduction

Many scholars have seen "Innovation" as a phenomenon for centuries serving the only purpose of improving the lives of human beings. It has been a paramount importance in the history that "supporting, generating and implementing innovation" is a crucial aspect not only for well-being of human race but also for survival of firms, industries, countries and population. The understanding about innovation and its impact on human welfare has considerably changed over the last decades. It was understood as "… implementation of a new or significantly improved product (good or service), or process, a new marketing method, or a new organizational method in business practices, workplace organization or external relations" (OECD, Eurostat 2005). In today's context, practitioners explained that the term innovation is, by nature, not attributed to any values and comprehensive covering the whole range of activities from discovery to first-time practical utilization of new knowledge of any kind which aims to fulfil the requirements and meeting the goals of end users in new ways.

Innovation is a key factor for economic growth and an essential element of industrial competitiveness. Innovation literature originates from various disciplines such as social sciences, psychology, management and economics and altogether applicable to a wide range of industry sectors and markets. The literature on innovation includes a broad set of definitions on innovation. Wolfe (1994) states that "innovation literature is a fragmented corpus, and scholars from diverse disciplinary backgrounds adopt a variety of ontological and epistemological positions to investigate, analyze and report on a phenomenon that is complex and multidimensional." A lack of agreement on a single definition to the term 'innovation' is commonly noted by several researchers in the literature (Yamin & Mavondo, 2015). Damanpour and Gopalakrishnan (1998) have also noted that different definitions of innovation tend to overlap and depend on an organization's environment. Literature on product development, process development, service development, and business development is considered to deal with key areas of innovation.

Although there have been a high number of studies related to innovation in last few decades, still there is no specific prescription for successful innovation (Rothwell, 1992). On the macro level, innovation has been identified as a cause of economic wealth (OECD, 2001). Meanwhile, it is considered as a continuum for the establishment of new or incremental change of products and/or processes leading to higher competitiveness in a micro level or at the firm level (Stock et al., 2002). This embraces inter and intra firm relationships across organizational boundaries to stimulate performance, build up competitive advantage, and enable market flexibility (Akamavi, 2005). Innovation is also instrumental in achieving the shortening of product life cycles for firms, and taking advantage of new opportunities (Barkema et al., 2002). The extent of innovation can range from incremental to radical. The former appears only at a micro level and results either in minor marketing or technological discontinuity (Porter, 1990). However, the latter has major marketing and technological discontinuity effects at both macro and micro levels (Garcia & Calantone, 2002).

The National Innovation Council defines innovation as: "Innovation today is increasingly going beyond the confines of formal R&D to redefine everything. Today innovation can mean new and unique applications of old technologies; using design to develop new products and services; new processes and structures to improve performance in diverse areas; organizational creativity; public sector initiatives to enhance delivery of services."

National Knowledge Commission (NKC) defines innovation in the following manner that "Innovation is defined as a process by which varying degrees of measurable value enhancement are planned and achieved, in any commercial activity. This process may be a breakthrough or incremental, and it may occur systematically in a company or sporadically; it may be achieved by introducing new or improved goods or services, operational processes and organizational or managerial processes in order to improve market share, competitiveness and quality, while reducing costs."

Innovation is the process of transforming creative ideas into useful applications through the deliberate efforts for combining resources in new or unusual ways to provide value to society by means of improved products, technology, or services. It involves creating, using the thing (inventions) in different dimensions, better way of doing things or an improvement. Innovation means "doing things differently, and doing different things, to create a step change in performance." Innovation is applying basic discoveries or inventions to produce a useful product or process for a specific application. Product innovation refers to the development of new and improved products or services, whereas the process innovation refers to new or improved methods of production or distribution. Innovations may not be patented, even though often times the distinction between inventions and innovations is blurry. Discoveries and inventions are rarely profitable in themselves. Innovation is necessary to bring the product to market economically. As the Patent Report observes, "Invention is the first step of innovation, but innovation often requires significant additional development activity beyond that first step in order to get new products and services to consumers."... Media, still casually refer to invention and innovation interchangeably.

Innovations can occur through any goal directed behaviors pertaining to profit maximization, philanthropism, authority, politics, individual aspiration and living styles. To turn an invention into an innovation, a firm typically needs to combine several different types of knowledge, capabilities, skills and resources from within the organization and the external environment. Telephone is an invention. Every innovation gave it new dimension like Touch-Tone Phone (old land line model), cordless phone, and mobile phones. Nowadays, "product innovation" is the centre of attention and reasonably well understood feature of the innovation phenomenon.

It is widely agreed in academia that service innovations are often overlooked and less attention is paid to explore their dimensions and development. One of the reasons why these service innovations were not being discussed widely in literature is that they don't look amaze to general public as compared with product innovation. Researchers in the innovation domain have to deal with the public imaginations that are in general identifying any form of innovation through inventions. Another form of innovation i.e. process innovation also has an significant impact on society. It is also widely acknowledged that the "Business Model Innovation" is the most significant of all four types of innovation as it dealt with the organisational change and social change in a simultaneous manner.

As per FICCI report on Innovation (2012) "Innovations in India had been largely the product centered. Not much thought has been applied to innovating business, marketing, and delivery processes that would give superior benefits to consumers. This focus is now changing. These days, world-class companies such as Microsoft, PepsiCo, IBM, Cisco, Nokia, GE, Xerox, and so on are using India as their research and development (R&D) base to pilot next-generation business models and organizational structures and to develop affordable and sustainable solutions that can then be marketed on a global scale. In doing so, these firms are synergistically integrating their India R&D operations into their global innovation networks. However, that is only one part of the story."

Innovation in India is basically driven by Indian entrepreneur and the progress in promoting innovation across the country is significant in terms of various phases of innovation viz. ideation, development of solutions, proof of concept, pilot production and commercial launch. India needs cultivate the innovation as a habit by involving efforts of every individual in the open innovation environment through a network of academic institutions, research organisations, industries and customers.

In literature a useful distinction is drawn between "radical innovation" and "incremental innovation." Radical innovations include "entirely new products," usually introduced by new business firms with the interdisciplinary knowledge base. Whereas the incremental innovations are the improvement or refinement of already existed products with new features and with new ways of usages introduced by the incumbent firm with a limited or specialized knowledge base.

At the root, inclusive innovation takes a different view of development from conventional views of innovation (IDRC 2011): "Conventional views of innovation (often implicitly) understand the development as generalized economic growth. By contrast, inclusive innovation explicitly conceives development in terms of active inclusion of those who are excluded from the mainstream of development. Differing in its foundational view of development, inclusive innovation, therefore, refers to the inclusion within some aspect of innovation of groups who are currently marginalized"

Aijay Govindarajan, Professor of International Business, Dartmouth College, USA stated that "Today, the locus of innovation in the global economy is shifting. Many multinationals are moving away from the traditional model of 'globalisation,' where they develop products in their wealthy developed nation and distribute them worldwide." In contrast to the globalisation, he observed a phenomenon called "Reverse Innovation" where the production took place in developing nations and then marketed to developed nations. Marketing innovation refers to the implementation of a "new marketing method involving significant changes in product design or packaging, product placement, product promotion or pricing." Organizational innovation involves "implementation of a new organizational method in the firm's business practices, workplace organization or external relations."

Over the period of last thirty years, innovation is evolved as the iconic term to represent the national economic development, technological status and business drivers of the country. Nowadays, innovation means not just the "creation of something new" but also a source for the solution of board range of problems. More and more exotic types of innovation start to develop like "blue ocean innovation" [Kim and Mauborgne, 2005], "frugal innovation" [Tiwari and Herstatt, 2011], and "organic innovation" [Moore, 2005]. The main subject of innovation is now not only the innovator himself but also such "archetypes" as "customer anthropologist" [GE and Stone Yamashita Partners, 2005] and "roadblock remover" or "innovation faces" like "cross-pollinator" and "caregiver" [Kelley and Littman, 2005].

The basic definitions and types of innovation (sometimes referred to as "shapes" or "typology" of innovation) are given by the Organization for Economic Cooperation and Development (OECD) in a series of manuals. The latest revision of these manuals is the Oslo Manual which defines innovation "the implementation of a new or significantly improved product (good or service), or process, a new marketing method, or a new organizational method in business practices, workplace organization or external relations" [OECD, 2005, p. 46]. An earlier OECD definition describes innovation as: "… all those scientific, technical, commercial and financial steps necessary for the successful development and marketing of new or improved manufactured products, the commercial use of new or improved processes or equipment or the introduction of a new approach to a Social service. R&D is only one of these steps." [OECD, 1981]. In these two examples, an evolution of the notion "innovation" becomes apparent. While in 1980s the focus was on steps of innovations, the main focus switched to innovation implementation and innovation typologies.

In general, there are two major aspects of innovation through which researchers distinguished innovation phenomenon as a process of change or as an event, object, product, etc. with novelty. However, since this classification is very broad, it can be split further. "Innovation as event, object or a discrete product" can be separated into several aspects: "innovation as event", "innovation as physical object" and "innovation as something new (new process or method for organization of something." Over the period of time, a more specific classification of innovation aspects was developed by Godin (2008) description of concepts of innovation as depicted in the following figure.

Figure 3.1 Various concepts on Innovation

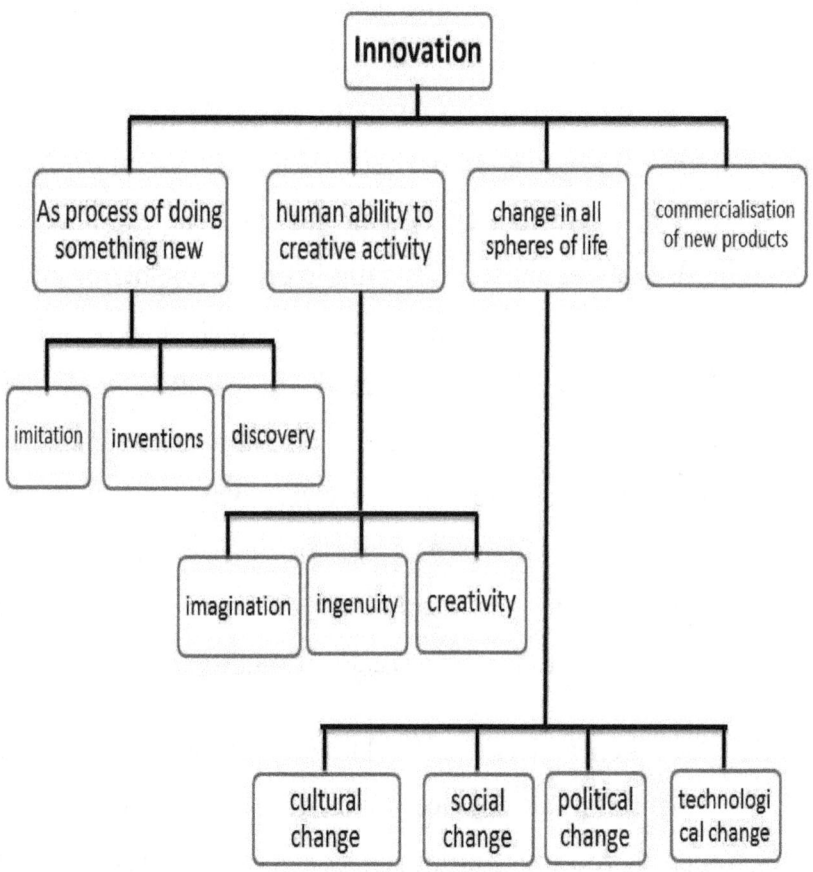

In literature, various characteristics of innovation are explained through various definitions by different scholars across the world. Different definitions reflect the broad spectrum of aspects of innovation. Barnett (1953) considers innovation as "something new of any thought, behaviour or thing that is new because it is qualitatively different from existing forms." Drucker (1985) and O'Sullivan & Dooley (2009) describes innovation as a "conduit of change - Innovation is the specific tool of entrepreneurs, the means by which they exploit change as an opportunity for a different business or a different service. It is capable of being presented as a discipline, capable of being learned, capable of being practiced." O'Sullivan & Dooley (2009) also describes innovation as "The application of practical tools and techniques that make changes, large and small, to products, processes, and services, which result in the introduction of something new for the organization and add value to the customers and contributes to the knowledge store of the organization."

Aiken and Hage (1971) see innovation as "… the generation, acceptance, and implementation of new ideas, processes, products, or services…. for the first time within an organization setting." Rasul (2003) defines innovation as "… the process whereby ideas for new (or improved) products, processes or services are developed and commercialized in the marketplace." Beyond the process dimension, Wang & Kafouros (2009) recognize innovation as a value driver: "Innovation through infusion of new products and services, and provide an impetus to emerging economies by opening up opportunities of international trade." Zaltman, Duncan and Holbek (1973) see innovation as invention: "… a creative process whereby two or more existing concepts or entities are combined in some novel way to produce a configuration not previously known by the person involved"

In their book "Innovation management: context, strategies, systems and processes" Ahmed and Shepherd (2010) defined six aspects of innovation. These aspects of innovation can be summarized as follows: innovation as something new (some real object: product, service or software); innovation as a process of doing, creating something new; innovation as the instrument for doing, creating something new; innovation as condition (environment) for doing something new; innovation as idea (concept) of something new; innovation as human abilities for doing something new; innovation as a process of change.

Several conceptual definitions of innovation were developed during 1960s. For example, Robertson (1967) defines innovation as "a process by which a new idea, behavior, or thing, which is qualitatively different from existing forms, is implemented and applied in practice." According to Mohr (1969), innovation can be a source for creating a new that can be developed product or process that is new to her followers (adoption unit)." These definitions reveal that during 1960s, innovation was interpreted mainly concerning "conceptual aspects" without taking into account the complexity and diversity of market and economies of different nations. Afterwards, during 1980s and 1990s, several methodological principles are proposed, which reflect the classification features of innovations such as "new to firm", "new to market" and "new to the world economy" (Kwon and Zmud, 1987; Bacon and Butler 1998).

Understanding the link between innovation and newness is important to visualize the phenomenon of innovation. According to Rogers` Definition, innovation is "an idea, practice, or object that is perceived as new by an individual or other unit of adoption." Further to develop the Rogers` Concept of re-invention, Walker in his research has synthesized the definition of innovation as "a process through which new ideas, objects, and practices are created, developed or reinvented and are new and novel to the unit of adoption."

Several researchers like Dakhli and de Clercq (2004) developed a hypothesis that "the changes associated with innovation should be considered in a social context in terms of their users." They argued that at an institutional level, all the innovations must be seen as social processes, not as scientific discoveries. In this view of innovation, it is possible to estimate the impact of innovation in the structures and procedures of organizations. The goal of innovation is to create value and positive impact on the organizations. Hence, innovation may need to include only the changes which have favourable consequences on organizations.

Among the concepts of innovation, the concept in which innovation is being perceived as a value driver is important for measuring the efficiency of innovation. In this concept, innovation is defined as a "source of competitive advantage" and is seen as a "decisive factor for economic growth" and the key requirement of company to survive in competitive environment (Johannessen, 2009). The adoption of innovation may lead to operational efficiency and create better working practices to ensure sustainable competitive advantage in dynamic market conditions. Following table summarizes the various important models of innovation discussed in the literature.

Literature on innovation process theory shares the varying relevance and importance for sources of innovation, which have changed considerably over the period of time and phases of innovation. It is also observed that the researchers' understanding is gradually shifted from the linear view to integrated view of the innovation process. This view of the innovation process emphasized that all the phases in an innovation process overlap with each other and facilitate the knowledge transfer among various sources for smooth innovation promotion with feedback from each phase. All of these innovation process approaches revolve around two basic approaches "Innovation management approach" and "Conceptual approach."

Table 1 Major Conceptual models on Innovation

Generation	Period	Authors of fundamental ideas	Innovation model	Essence of the model
1	1950s-1960s		Technology push	Linear process
2	Late 1960s-first half of 1970s	Myers and Marquis, 1969	Market (need) pull	R&D on customer wishes
3	Second half of 1970s-end of 1980s	Mowery and Rosenberg, 1979	Coupling model	Interaction of different functions
		Rothwell and Zegveld, 1985	Interactive model	Interaction with research institutions and market
4	End of 1980s – early 1990s	Kline and Rosenberg, 1986	Integrated model	Simultaneous process with feedback loops: "chain linked model"
5	1990s	Rothwell, 1992	Networking model	System integration and networks (SIN)
6	2000s	Chesbrough, 2003	Open Innovation	Innovation collaboration and multiple exploitation paths
7	2010s		Open innovator	Focus on the individual and framework conditions under which to become innovative

19

The "innovation management" approach focuses on firm's management strategies in governing the innovation process in view of the firm socio-economic and political circumstances rather than concentrating on the models of the innovation process. Some of the exemplary research work on innovation management approach includes Rothwell (1994), Niosi (1999), Verloop (2004), Cagnazzo, Botarelli and Taticchi (2008), Jacobs and Snijders (2008), Eveleeens (2010). The "conceptual approach" relies on the conceptual essence of the innovation models and analyzes the theoretical issues of such models in terms of their advantages and disadvantages. Marinova and Phillimore (2003) provided the comprehensive analysis of various innovation models referred in the literature. "Innovation system" model was greatly addressed with a wide of conceptual researchers in recent times.

After conceiving the knowledge as one of the crucial factors of production and witnessing its deterministic impact on economic growth rate of various nations in the world, researchers have been trying to understand this phenomenon through the innovation window. Our understanding about the innovation process has undergone through various transitional stages. To have an exponential understanding about our efforts to conceptualize and theorize the process of innovationdevelopment, it is necessary to observe the phenomenal research work in this discipline. One best way to achieve this task is to explore the research work across different generations of research efforts in understanding innovation phenomenon. In the early 1990s, Rothwell (1992) described five generations of innovation models: ***technology push; need pull; coupling model*** (with feedback loops); ***integrated model*** (with simultaneous links between R&D, prototyping and manufacturing) and ***systems integration/networking model*** (with emphasis on strategic linkages between firms). The approach taken in this section to present an overview of innovation literature reflects a similar chronology explained by *Dora Marinova and John Phillimore (2003);* however, it extends Rothwell's typology. In this section, a detailed note is presented on six generations of innovation models, namely: First generation—***the black box model***; Second generation—***linear models*** (including technology push and need pull); Third generation—***interactive models*** (including coupling and integrated models); Fourth generation—

systems models (including networking and national systems of innovation); Fifth generation—***evolutionary models***; and Sixth generation—***innovative milieux***.

First Generation Conceptualisation:

The Black Box Model

It is evident from the world history is that there are variations in country's economic growth rates and the growth patterns. Since the technological factor was included in the production function to explain the variations in economic performance of the countries by Solow, researchers have been trying to explore the phenomenon with various approaches. According to Solow, the component of economic growth, which could not be explained by the changes in labour and capital, is due to the technological advances. He concluded that about 90% of the per capita output could be attributed to technological change. Inadequate knowledge about what will happen when invest on science and technology leads to the emergence of the black box model.

Despite its significant role in the economic development, technological phenomenon was treated as the events that inside a black box. Although several economists have recognized the importance of of this transitional process, "the economics profession has adhered rather strictly to a self-imposed ordinance not to inquire too seriously into what transpires inside that box" (Rosenberg, 1982, p. vii). Although it does not explain research and development characteristics, it draws attention to the fact that "firms and industries that spend relatively large amounts on R&D may tend to have managements that are relatively progressive and forward looking" (Mansfield, 1995, p. 259). The black box when coupled with the appropriate and timely management activities makes certain firms more successful than others.

Second Generation Conceptualisation:

Linear Models

In 1960s and 1970s, researchers interested in the specific processes that generate new technologies and the learning involved in technological change with which they have tried to open the black box of innovation. The expectations were that understanding innovation would also open the road to formulating policies that stimulate R&D and consequently, lead to the development of new products and processes. Innovation was perceived as a step by step process, as a sequence of activities that lead to the technologies being adopted by the markets. The first linear description of innovation was given by the so called 'technology push' model, which was closely related to the 'science push' model of science policy advocated by Vannevar Bush in his ground breaking 'Science: The Endless Frontier' report. According to that report, discoveries in basic science eventually lead to technological developments, which result in a flow of new products and processes to the market place (Rothwell & Zegveld, 1985, p. 49). The step sequence is as follows:

Basic Science ⇒ Applied Science and Engineering ⇒ Manufacturing ⇒ Marketing ⇒ Sales

This model is not confined to these stages only, there may be variations across organisations and industries (Beije, 1998 or Feldman, 1994), but the focus is on technological newness as a driving force for innovation. The 'technology push' model is also associated with the name and theoretical work of Schumpeter, who studied the role of the entrepreneur as the person taking the risk and overcoming the barriers in order to extract the monopolistic benefits from the introduction of new ideas (Coombs et al., 1987).

The linear 'need pull' or 'market driven' model was developed after realization of the market power to induce demand for new goods and services. In recognition of the importance of the marketplace and the demands of potential consumers of technology, it states that the causes of innovation are existing demands so that the step sequence becomes as follows (Rothwell & Zegveld, 1985). The main exponent of demand-led innovation is considered to be Schmookler, who studied patterns in patents and investments (Coombs et al., 1987; Hall, 1994). His conclusion was that fluctuations in investments in innovation can be explained better by external events (e.g. demand) than by trends in inventive activities (e.g. essence of technology).

> **Market Place ⇒ Technology Development ⇒ Manufacturing ⇒ Sales**

The 1960s and 1970s witnessed an enormous amount of research on success factors for innovation. The technology-push/need-pull dichotomy was used to explain not only a wide range of successfully introduced new technologies but also numerous cases of failure.

Third Generation Conceptualisation: Interactive Models

Linear models were regarded as an extremely simplified picture of the generally complex interactions between science, technology and the market. There was a need for deeper understanding and a more thorough description of all the aspects and actors of the innovation process. The sequential nature of innovation was questioned and the process was subdivided into separate stages, each of them interacting with the others. According to Rothwell and Zegveld (1985, p. 50), "the overall pattern of the innovation process can be thought of as a complex net of communication paths, both intra-organizational and extra-organizational, linking together the various in-house functions and linking the firm to the broader scientific and technological community and to the marketplace." The stages are as follows (Rothwell, 1983):

Figure 3.2 Rothwell model of innovation

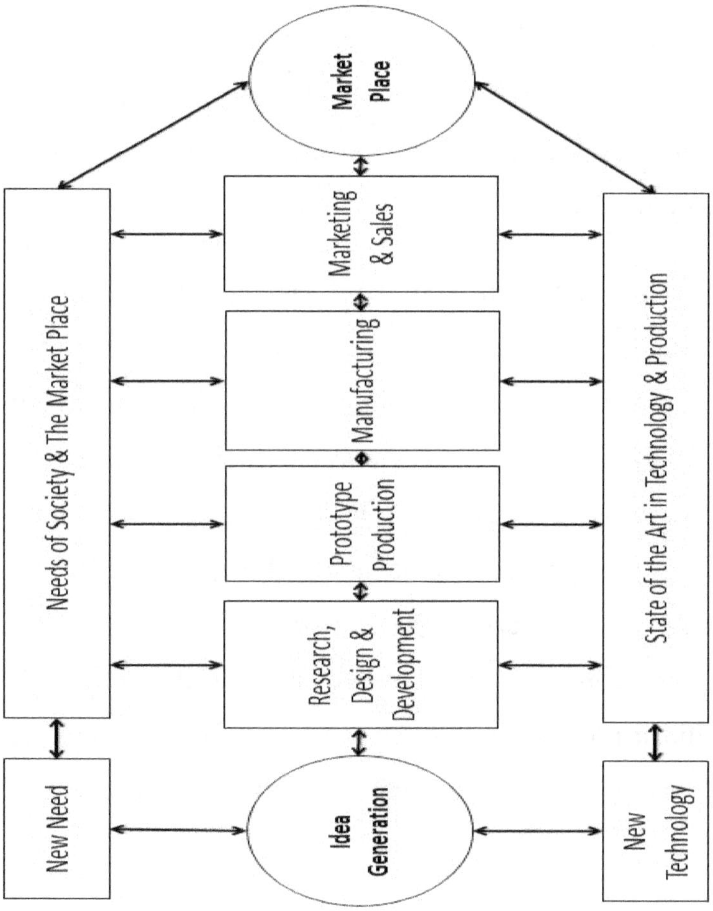

In this interactive model, innovation is no longer the end product of a final stage of activity but can occur at various places throughout the process (Beiji 1998). It can also be circular and iterative rather than sequential. An example of this was the 'chain-link' model suggested by Kline & Rosenberg (1986) which includes feedbacks and loops allowing potential innovators to seek existing inter- and intra-firm knowledge as well as carry out or commission additional research to resolve any problems arising from the market design-production-distribution process.

The interactive model was an attempt to bring together the technology-push and market-pull approaches into a comprehensive model of innovation. As a result, it provided a more complete and comprehensive approach to the issue of the factors and players involved in innovation. However, it still did not explain what drives the engine of innovation and why some companies are better at doing it than others. Nor did it provide an answer as to how organizations learn or what is the role of their operational environment.

Fourth Generation Conceptualisation:

System Models

The most well-known system model is the so-called national systems of innovation (e.g. Freeman, 1991; Lundvall, 1992; Nelson, 1993, 2000). It deals with the diversity in approaches to innovation in countries around the globe which differ in size, level of economic development, historical traditions or level of concern about specific policy problems (e.g. education or global warming). According to one study, this is reflected in the way the main actors in the innovation process (firms, public and private research organizations, government and other public institutions) interact and the forms, quality and intensity of these interactions (OECD, 1999, p. 22). A national system of innovation is defined as a set of institutions, which jointly and individually contribute to the development and diffusion of new technologies and provide a framework for the implementation of government policies influencing the innovation process (Metcalfe, 1995).The The most important feature of this set is its interconnectedness, the way the various elements interact.

Fifth Generation Conceptualisation:

Evolutionary Models

The need for an evolutionary approach in economics was proposed based on failures in neoclassical economics, including its inability to deal with dynamic qualitative changes, which are internal features of technological innovation (Saviotti 1996, p. 29). Hodgson (1993) argues that the mechanical metaphor adopted in orthodox economic thinking has the weak explanatory power, as economics and innovation are products of living creatures. Hence, the biological metaphor is more useful and parallels can be made with the Darwinian evolution of species. More recently, evolutionary studies of technological change have combined fundamentals not only from biology, but also from equilibrium thermodynamics, organizational theory and heterodox approaches in economics. According to Saviotti (1996), following are the key concepts in an evolutionary approach to innovation:

• Generation of variety—innovation process is generally seen as equivalent to mutation development.

They continuously generate new products, processes and forms and hence increase the variety in the system. Not all mutations (new technological developments) are successful, but the ones, which often replaces older products and processes consequently making them extinct.

• Selection—selection processes act together with variety-generating mechanisms. The outcome is the 'survival' (which could also be interpreted as introduction or maintenance) of some products, technologies and firms as a result of their adaptation to the environment in which they operate, and the demise of others.

• Reproduction and inheritance—firms are perceived as producing organizations and inheritance is expressed in the continuity in which organizations take decisions, develop products and generally do their business. Firms are learning entities, but any developed expertise is difficult to inherit or transfer to other firms.

• Fitness and adaptation—Darwin's 'survival of the fittest' principle is represented by the propensity of an economic unit to be successful in a given environment.

- Population perspective—variation is an essential component for an evolutionary process. Hence, not only average values but also variances in the population of firms/products should be analyzed.

- Elementary interactions—these include mainly competition (between products or firms) and are the most studied interaction in economics. More recently, collaboration has also become a recognized type of interaction.

- External environment— a key element in the evolutionary approach. It traditionally covers the socioeconomic (including regulatory) environment in which technologies are developed. It is determined by mechanisms such as patent regimes, market structures, standards and regulations. More recently (in the case of the green or ecologically friendly technologies) it has also started to include the link with the natural environment.

Nelson & Winter (1982) were the first to translate the conceptual evolutionary model into a computer simulation model describing business behaviour based on the so-called 'routines' or regular and predictable behavioural patterns and habits of firms. This model was initially applied to data used by Solow (1957) who studied U.S. productivity. Nelson and Winter were successful in demonstrating that 'realistic' firm behaviour could account for macroeconomic outcomes at least as well as Solow's growth modelling production function. With the further advance of computer technologies, the 1980s and 1990s witnessed further interest in evolutionary modelling (Kwasnicki, 2000).

The evolutionary model stresses 'bounded rationality' (Dosi & Egibi, 1991) and the value of diversity (Dowrick, 1995). It also shows how, under meaningful economic values of certain parameters, such as technological opportunities, and established decision-making rules, firms can be dynamic self-organized systems (Dosi & Orsenigo, 1994). The selection process and the importance of the surrounding environment shed light on the processes of failure of generally fit technologies and the success of technologies, which are considered inferior (e.g. MSDOS computer operation system or VHS video recording system). According to Tisdell (1995) "a fit technique. . . may fail to be selected because its surrounding environment at the time of its occurrence is unfavorable." According to Bryant & Wells (1998), the evolutionary school of thought is likely to become very influential in policy considerations. Since World War II, governments have consistently funded outcome oriented research. What the evolutionary model emphasizes is that the process is as (if not more) important as the results from R&D. For example, a 1996 OECD report recommends governments to increase the population of innovative firms as a main policy goal rather than correcting market failure (OECD, 1996).

The evolutionary model also points out that, outcomes are to a large degree determined by the evolutionary process, be it at the level of company or country. Shedding light on how decisions are made and how the various participants interact to produce innovations, is a major explanatory feature of this model. Therefore, governments should be urged to create conditions conducive to the process of innovation by shaping relationships, encouraging learning, and balancing competition with cooperation.
The model has a less normative power, and is less focused on the implications for innovation strategy at the level of the firm beyond the need for firms to

protect diversity and a range of competencies (of people, product ranges, technologies, etc.).

Related to the evolutionary model are a number of generalizations, which appeared in the 1970s and 1980s. They refer to technological imperatives (Rosenberg, 1976), innovation avenues (Sahal, 1981), technological trajectories (e.g. Biondi & Galli, 1992; Pavitt et al., 1989), technological (Dosi, 1982, 1988) and technoeconomic paradigms (Freeman & Perez, 1988; Perez, 1983). The main argument is that during a particular time period, we witness certain regularities in the development of technologies (represented by the nature of the applied principles and practical solutions), but they are often hindered by the delays with which institutions adapt to the new potential of these technologies.

In addition to explanatory power, an extremely important aspect of any model is its predictive potential. If a model is a relatively accurate representation of reality, the traditional scientific approach expects it to deliver forecasts and predictions of future parameter values. The evolutionary model, in general, lacks such a capacity as it describes a constant change and hence its parameters are always in flux. Nevertheless, there is some degree of predictability if we can explain the mechanisms supporting the continuity of the old and the introduction of the new and if we can characterize the turning points in between.

Sixth Generation Conceptualisation:

Innovative Milieux

Since the 1970s, a large body of literature has developed dealing with aspects of the growth of regional clusters of innovation and high technology (Feldman, 1994; Keeble & Wilkinson, 2000). The importance of geographical location for knowledge generation gave rise to the innovative milieux explanatory model. The concept is the main contribution by geographers, regional economists and urban planners to a field, which traditionally has been studied by economists and sociologists. The real-estate rule of: 'Location! Location! Location!' started to attract attention to the natural, social and built environment surrounding establishments where technologies are developed. The model includes networking and linkages but goes beyond that to emphasize the importance of quality-of-life factors.

The innovative milieu model states that "innovation stems from a creative combination of generic know how and specific competencies" and "territorial organization is an essential component of the process of techno-economic creation" (Bramanti & Ratti, 1997, p. 5). According to Longhi & Keeble (2000, p. 27), "the innovation process is not spaceless. On the contrary, innovation seems to be an intrinsically territorial, localized phenomenon, which is highly dependent on resources, which are location specific, linked to specific places and impossible to reproduce elsewhere." An early description of innovative milieux by Camagni (1991) lists the following components:

- A productive system, e.g. innovative firm.
- Active territorial relationships, e.g. inter-firm and inter-organizational interactions fostering innovation
- Different territorial socio-economic actors, e.g. local private or public institutions supporting innovation
- A specific culture and representation process

- Dynamic local collective learning process.

Camagni & Capello (2000) emphasize that the interactions creating the innovative milieu are not necessarily based on market mechanisms but include movement and exchange of goods, services, information, people and ideas among others. They are not always formalized in cooperative agreements or any other contracts. Major features of such an environment are the ease of contact and trust between partners, which reduce uncertainty in the development of new technologies and prove to be a source of exchange of tacit knowledge. In addition to the components of a productive working environment, more recently other factors have started to impact on the capacity of locations to generate innovative firms. They relate to the social, cultural and natural characteristics of the place, such as proximity to recreational sites, climate and air quality, quality of life for family members, including children, to mention a few. The high density of links is also being expressed in relation to interactions with the local community (Willoughby, 1995).

The innovation milieu concept explains the success of small and medium-sized enterprises, which, in general, lack the resources to maintain aggressive R&D strategies and operate at the cutting edge of technologies. The existing supporting network compensates for that and provides an operational "microcosm in which all those elements which are traditionally considered as the sources of economic development and change within the firm operate as if they were *in vitro*" (Camagni & Capello, 2000, p. 120). The model also explains why certain localities give birth to a large number of small innovative firms, which are situated in close proximity and share a similar cultural and business ethos. It also highlights the fact that different localities have different patterns and paths in knowledge development and transfer of high technology.

Porter's (1990) analysis of groups of firms located in geographic proximity is often referred to as 'innovation clusters'. According to the OECD (1999), the concept of clusters is closely linked to firms networking but it goes beyond that as it captures all forms of knowledge sharing and exchange within a specific locality. Many clusters have developed over extended periods of time and have deep historical roots. Often they are also linked to the particular natural, human and other resources available in the region. Other closely related concepts are 'the learning region' (Florida, 1995; Kirat & Lung, 1999; Macleod, 1996; Simmie, 1977) and 'collective learning' (Keeble, 2000; Lawson, 2000). They stress that learning is the most important feature of any economy and successful regions provide particular combinations of institutions and organizations to encourage knowledge development within the community and learning by local firms through conscious and unconscious mechanisms.

The innovative milieux model has not so far addressed the links between innovation and ecology. It is still predominantly anthropocentric, and innovators rarely address the issues of harmony with the natural environment. Nevertheless, there is increasing evidence that the development of technologies is not a means of its own but a mechanism to achieve broader goals. An example of this is the Finnish environmental cluster research program (Honkasado, 2000), which covers projects encouraging cooperation between entrepreneurs who utilize the natural environment for eco-business and promote innovative enterprises specializing in environmental technologies. The interest in the locality will hopefully result in increased consideration of issues such as ecologically sustainable development and social justice.

In management context, many scholars have defined the term 'innovation' from various perspectives. Rogers (2004) defines innovation as "any idea or practice or object that is perceived to be new by an individual or other unit of adoption" consisting of certain technical knowledge about how things can be done better than the existing state of the art. In other words, innovation is related to the adoption of new products and/or processes to increase competitiveness and overall profitability (Tyler, 2001).

Menrad (2004) similarly viewed innovation as a complex phenomenon related to production, diffusion and translation of scientific or technical knowledge to new or modified products/services including new production or processing techniques. Francis and Bessant (2005) add that innovation is not only about the changes or so-called new things based on individual perception, but it is also linked to achieving a better market position, a new way to introduce a product in a new context, or a business model or a new method to find new challenges and opportunities, which are related to market exploitation. In line with the study of Porter (1990), innovation is considered as a new approach to doing things commercially.

Lundvall (2010) further interprets innovation as an on-going process leading to four different outcomes including new products, new techniques, new forms of organisation and new markets. It is derived from the interrelationship between product, process and organisational innovativeness and market identification. Product innovativeness is defined as activities leading to any product, service or idea that is recognised by someone as new based upon individual perception (Danneels & Kleinschmidtb 2001). Meanwhile, process innovativeness could be the adaptation of an existing production system, which can be either steadily or radically achieved.

The implementation of a new production technology, for example, is a result of process innovativeness (Utterback 1971). Organisational innovativeness involves changes in workplace organisation such as marketing, purchasing, sales administration, management and staff policy (Clarysse & Bruneel, 2007). The penetration of new market segments and the exploitation of new territorial markets within an existing market sector is an output of market identification.

In short, innovation is basically identified as the main factor that boosts the competitiveness and economic growth of all industries. The definitions of innovations are scattered and varied, depending on different ontological and epistemological positions. In the view of management studies, innovation is considered as something new to an individual, mostly defined in the form of products or processes leading to an increase of firms' competitiveness. In a broader context, innovation is regarded as an on-going process leading to the development of new processes, products, organization and new markets.

It is important to note that the surge in the intensity of competition has been accompanied with an increase in the number of organizations that have realized that it is not enough that firms improve organizational efficiencies, but they should also explore the role of innovation as a driver of sustainable competitive advantages. It should be noted that both Solo (1951) and Schumpeter (1982) had predicted that competitive advantages might be linked to intensive technological innovations. In recent times, Yeung (1999) argued that competition, which was a key driver for competitive advantages, might also be a driver for innovation. From these perspectives, it emerges that there are two important relationships that exist out of competitiveness.

The first is the link between competition and globalization (Hamel & Prahalad, 1985) and the other is the link between competition and innovation (Yeung, 1999). Although most of the published work in the literature is concerned with issues related to innovation-driven competition, the role of globalization as a driver to innovation is largely ignored. In other words, the model by Yeung (1999) points to a possible link between competition and innovation, while the work of Hamel and Prahalad (1985) proposes a link between competition and globalization. This means that the models of Hamel and Prahalad (1985) and Yeung (1999) may share a number of factors that are mutually inclusive factors. This mutual inclusivity may, in fact, point to the possibility that globalization could be a possible common to both competition and innovation. Figure 1 illustrates the interrelationship which will form a possible research direction.

Already, in 1986 Tushman & Nadler stressed that "organisations can gain competitive advantage only by managing effectively for today while simultaneously creating innovation for tomorrow" and suggested that "there is perhaps no more pressing managerial problem that the sustained management of innovation." Tushman & Nadler (1986) identify visionary leadership and also people, structures and values as important factors that affect whether an organization realizes benefits from innovation. Innovation is still seen as a critical drive of economic performance.

Martín-de Castro et al. (2013) say that developing successful technological innovations is essential for creating and sustaining an organisation´s competitive advantage. According to Zemplinerová (2010) the expenditures on research, development and introduction of innovations are the determining characteristics for gaining a dominant part of the market. Autant-Bernard, Fadairo & Massard (2013) in their survey also show the importance of the role of the regional innovation and they argue that organisation must have original strategies and support the knowledge flows from and to organisation. It is supported by results of Noruzy et al. (2012) and Autant-Bernard (2001).

The above paragraphs showed that the innovative activity of the organisations significantly influences the competitiveness, which is based on inimitable skills and abilities. Achieving a higher competitiveness, by innovations, means producing low cost products with better quality when compared with those manufactured by competitors. If an organisation is not capable of introducing innovations on an ongoing basis will lag behind, and such initiatives will be taken over by other entities. Schumpeter (in Tidd et al., pp. 8, 2006) asserts that entrepreneurs attempt to use technological innovation – a new product or service or perhaps a new process in the course of their production – to gain a strategic competitive advantage. This creates competition that does not attack profit margins or the outputs of existing organisations, but their essence and their existence as such.

With respect to the above aspects it is important that there is a necessity in today's knowledge, information and innovative society to follow large organisations that engage in innovation and set the direction for others (Zemplinerová, 2010). The present concept of innovations is that they represent an open approach that reaches beyond the threshold of an organisation and thus exploits not only inspections and changes in the internal environment, but also changes in the external environment.

The internal environment of an organisation needs to have a suitably present innovative culture, since this type of culture is characterised by the transience of organisational structures, utilisation of specialists and temporary teams, mobile offices, the necessity of speedy and flexible changes responding to new opportunities, which increases the innovative potential of such organisations (Molina-Morales et al. (2011).

There is no place for standardisation; each project is unique. Its characteristic features include flexibility, openness to changes, searching for information and resources in the external environment, anticipation, creativity, experimenting and informal communication. Checks in organisations with this type of culture are not necessary and in order to maintain consistency between managerial practices and the content of such culture it is actually impossible – good work is associated with loyalty arising from the engagement of employees in the fulfillment of the organisation's goals and performance of their tasks (Lukášová, 2010).

Companies must innovate in order to keep its position ahead of their competitors. If an organisation wants to create a business strategy that keeps it at the forefront of innovation, it must develop ways of making that strategy work. Being innovative does not just involve using the expertise of market researchers, scientists and product developers to create new products. It also involves using the capabilities of everyone within an organisation to generate the processes that help the new product to reach the market quickly and efficiently. It is after all people who innovate and not companies, and they need the right environment which provides both support and encouragement.

So why are some companies becoming more successful innovators than others? One theory about culture contrasts defender and prospector organisations probably anwere these questions. The defender culture resists change and favours strategies that provide security. This is usually supported by a bureaucratic style of management. On the other hand, a prospector organisation thrives on change and innovation. It differentiates its products in a creative and flexible working regime.

Chapter 2:

Innovation Management

In general, Innovation management refers to all the activities involved in innovation development and commercialization processes. In management context, it can be understood as the organizational strategies & actions that aimed at the development and promotion of innovation and appropriate of commercial returns from such innovations. Burgelman et al. (2004) defined innovation management as "a comprehensive set of characteristics of a firm that facilities and supports its strategies in innovation development and in appropriating the benefits/returns of innovation for sustainable competitive advantage."

Another model of innovation management proposed by Dogson (2000) includes six specific areas of innovation management. According to him, innovation management is a holistic model which includes various innovation activities like Research and Development; technological collaboration and technology strategy; operations and production; new-product development; commercialization of innovation. He also points out that the context of "Management of Technology

Innovation" is complex and risky. This process is associated with uncertainty, knowledge appropriation and costs unpredictability. As a result, firms require knowledge management and organizational skills in order to expertise in the innovation management process. Firms are not required to have very new and cutting-edge technologies to create innovation in the business. In practice, it is appeared that the innovation management is more of planning, coordinating, organising and controlling of organisational efforts to find creative solutions to the business problem. In this context, innovation management techniques (IMTs) can be seen as a "range of tools, techniques and methodologies that help companies to adapt to circumstances and meet market challenges in a systematic way" (Phaal et al., 2006). IMTs are the results of a new way of thinking and not necessarily due to technology, but more to the capacity of business organisation in make use of their knowledge and other resources in improving business and in maintaining relations with external actors.

Due to the variations in organisational resource profile and the context in which the business is operating, it is very difficult to evolve a set of innovation management techniques that suits to all kinds of organisational problems. In practice, it is impossible to claim that the particular innovation management techniques which resolved certain problems in the past may be useful to solve the present and future business problem. Hence, it is understood that innovation management techniques are context specific in which all the sources and actors of innovation are aligned according to the business and market requirements.

Innovation management techniques always need to be evaluated in combination with organisation context and cannot be considered in isolation. Organisation tries to mix up the innovation management techniques at varying degrees to tackle the specific business challenge with specific combination of innovation management techniques. The outcome of innovation management activities in any company determined by the choices of innovation management techniques and nature of the business organisation. The complementarity results from such a mix of innovation management techniques and nature of the organisation lead to faster and smooth innovation process. This requires the clear understanding about firm's objectives, activities, resources, challenges, business processes, market competitiveness, etc.

Chapter 3:

Innovation Management as a source of Competitive Advantage

These measurements are, nonetheless, considered as an imperfect measure of innovation performance in some innovation studies, since some companies may not conduct formal R&D activities and record new innovations via the patenting process (Bougrain & Haudeville, 2002). Rather than conducting formal experimental R&D, SMEs are often prone to rely upon the use of known scientific principles that they adapt to producing new innovations on an informal basis (Avermaete et al., 2003).

On the other hand, a broad range of innovation indicators, such as the number of new innovations and revenue attributed to new innovations, has become more and more important in capturing the level of innovation performance of a firm in recent innovation studies, whereby an innovative firm is assumed to develop more new innovations (i.e. new products and/or new processes) than a non-innovative firm (Wan et al. 2005). It is worth noting that firms tend to develop new innovations based upon the influence of factors such as changes in demand and competition in the market, improvement of production quality and delivery time, organisational change, and regulatory requirements (OECD 2005).

The common inputs which stimulate innovations in firms are research and development (R&D), normally represented by an expenditure towards R&D activities and/or degree of R&D orientation, funding, equipment (i.e. use of equipment related to innovation projects), and human resources (i.e. level of commitment from employees) (Greve, 2003). Brewin et al. (2009) have mentioned that it is in-house R&D, particularly, that has a direct positive impact on innovation performance of firms, based on the empirical evidence from more than 100 Canadian food-processing firms. Meanwhile, Sawyerr et al. (2003) and Temtime (2004) added that firms, especially SMEs, must make effective use of market scanning or external sources of knowledge as an innovation input to become successful in the development of new innovations.

It should be highlighted that R&D is no longer the sole means for explaining innovation processes (Raymond & St-Pierre 2010), since it often only reflects the innovation capacity of large enterprises, which are mostly R&D intensive sectors (Narula, 2004). Cebon, Newton and Nobel (1999) and Dodgson and Hinze (2000) found that high levels of R&D intensity may not necessarily indicate good innovation practice; this may simply complicate the innovation process. Equally significantly, other innovation inputs such as the development of marketing methods and organisational strategies, market identification, and acquisition of external knowledge have been found to play an equally important role in firm innovativeness, especially for SMEs since most of them are low to medium technology firms, where innovation is often driven by non R&D based activities (Santamaria et al., 2009).

On the other hand, the innovation outputs or business performances that resulted from innovations are commonly measured by a firm's turnover, impacts of innovation towards competition and demand in market (i.e. increase of market share), production (i.e. improved quality of goods and services, increase of production volume), and organisation (i.e. improved communication and interaction among different business activities) (OECD, 2005).

Firms that deal with uncertain business environment, through the development of innovation, outperform those firms that neglect on the innovation development (Garg et al., 2003). Thornhill (2006) statistically confirms this notion when he finds a positive linkage between innovation and firm performance, measured by revenue growth using the case of 845 Canadian manufacturing firms. Likewise, Gunday et al. (2011) identified the same association between different types of innovations by using a different measure of firm performance consist of marketing, production and financing performances in a study on 184 production organisations in Turkey. These factors, whether innovation inputs or innovation outputs, are linked and are involved in the management of innovation knowledge.

In the literature, several reasons are being claimed to failure of the organisations due to inefficient innovation management practices in terms of "managerial incompetence, organisational inertia, and insufficient technological intelligence" (Iansiti, 2000). Utterback and Suarez (1993) have mentioned that understanding technological trends at the sector level is considered important to firms since the successful firm adapts its innovation strategy to the phase of the sectoral product cycle and the temporal dynamics of technological production in specific industries. Other authors emphasize the essential ability of companies to tackle the change induced from innovations (Thomke & Kuemmerle, 2000) or highlighted the human resource importance and organisational routines to facilitate such change initiatives for organisational benefit (Nelson & Winter, 2009).

Brown and Eisenhardt (1998) similarly underlined that, since innovation is not a straightforward process or mechanically-driven, firms have to adapt and evolve with shifting competition and varying climate. Drucker (1994) argues that innovation management knowledge is the only way to convert change into opportunities. Firms which possess a higher level of innovation management capability tend to have a higher chance of becoming successful in their businesses compared to their less innovative peers, as they are more capable of dealing with the complexity of the innovation process (Tidd et al., 1997)."

This kind of various views showed that our understanding of innovation management has a strong linkage with firms' competitive advantage and highlighted the innovation management capability which builds on the other dynamic capabilities like R&D capability, organisational strategic capability, human-resource management capability, investment capability, resource allocation capability, production capability, etc. The more elaborate discussion on firm dynamic capabilities is presented in the next section.

Chapter 4:
Dynamic Capability

In literature, several researchers have expressed their concerns about the competition in business environment and its effect on firms' competitive advantage. Hallegren et al. (2011) suggested that to secure competitive advantage, which is being nullified due to intense competition, firms must deploy all kinds of capabilities to develop dynamic capability at all levels to tackle such turbulent situations. Firms demonstrates first-order dynamic capabilities through the changes in organizational processes to deal with demand volatility, but the second-order dynamic capabilities demonstrated to quickly reconfigure the resource base to change the nature of activities or to abort the implementation of current strategies (Harrigan, 1985).

Similar views are also given by Kazozcu (2011) that in turbulent environments, firms need to develop a unique set of resources to build competitive advantage. This unique set of resources built into skills and capabilities which are referred as core competences. However, in the changing nature of the environment, these core competences cannot remain static and necessitates continuous renovation. The ability to upgrade and reinvent these core competencies dynamically brings strategic flexibility in organisations.

"The concept of capabilities is not new as it was first proposed by Penrose (1959), who suggested that resources are comprised of a bundle of potential services. While these resources are available to all firms, the capability to assemble, integrate, and deploy them effectively is heterogeneously distributed in industry (Schendel, 1994)." Poulis and Jackson (2007) argued that the nature and creation of dynamic capabilities not only depend on the idiosyncratic characteristics of the frim, but also on external complexity in the business environment.

Companies could use these dynamic capabilities as weapons in the war against uncertainty and complexity of external environment. Zelbst et al. (2010) contended that "adoption of market orientation combined with JIT, TQM, and agile manufacturing programs leads to organizational capabilities of relatively low cost operation, relatively high-quality product and service production, and relatively rapid response to changes in customer needs and demand." Thus, dynamic capabilities reflect organisational ability in the achievement of competitive advantage in a given path dependencies and market positions (Leonard-Barton, 1992).

Dynamic capabilities are a set of unique and recognizable processes in organisations such as product development, strategic decision making, networking, etc. and are neither vague nor tautological. "Fan et al. (2009) summarized the aspects of dynamic capabilities as the competencies that allow a firm to quickly reconfigure its organizational structure and routines in response to new opportunities. They discussed the dynamic capabilities that are related with cost reduction, outsourcing, knowledge networking and knowledge management."

Tony Davila et al. (2012) classified dynamic capability in to "Financial Management Capability, Product Development Capability, Human Resource Management Capability, Strategic Planning Capability, Sales and Marketing Capability, Partnership Management Capability." Ho *et al.* (2011) examined the influence of technological capabilities and design capabilities on technology commercialization and observed that both technological and design capabilities have shown positive influence on technology commercialization.

Chapter 5:

The evolution of the dynamic capabilities concept

The dynamic capability concept is founded theoretically in Resource-Based View and Evolutionary Theory with its emphasis on routines and processes (Helfat and Peteraf 2009). These two foundations are discussed in the next sections before elaborating on capabilities and dynamic capability as an emerging theory.

5.1 The Resource-Based View

"Penrose (1959) in a significant departure from the neoclassical economics of the time proposed that the configuration of the resources possessed by a firm was the key source of competitive advantage in relation to firm growth: "if we want to explain why different firms see the same environment differently, why some grow and some do not....then we must take the resources approach" (Penrose, 1959). Economic theory at that time held that firms were largely homogenous entities operating in markets in search of equilibrium.

Economic theory did not generally consider the differences which existed between firms or did it attempts to include the actions of individual managers or entrepreneurs in its theories. Helfat and Peteraf (2009) argue that "it is an understatement to say that economic theory underplays the role of the manager; in fact, the strategic manager simply does not exist in any recognizable form."

Penrose proposed that it was the manner in which firms utilize their resources and services, they could deliver, paramount importance, rather than the simple existence or otherwise of the resources themselves. She defined resources to include both the physical resources available to a firm and the human resources employed and available to the firm. Penrose also found that there was an interrelation between the physical and human resources which influenced the productive services of the firms. Clearly, the physical resources present shape to the services which management might be capable of delivering. However, Penrose (1959) also held that "...the experience of management will affect the productive services that all its other resources are capable of rendering."

This recognition of the critical role of the management pervades Penrose's work and is central to the theory development. Penrose also found that the image which the firm's managers held of their own firm and the environment in which the firm operated was a critical issue in relation to the decisions which those managers would take. Wernerfelt (1984) seemed to synthesize Penrose (1959) and Porter's (1990) contributions when he argues for examining firms from a resource perspective rather than a product perspective. Building on this concept, Barney (2001) proposed four indicators in relation to resources (value, rareness, imitability and substitutability) which are all required if a resource is to deliver a sustained competitive advantage to a firm.

In his thesis, Barney (2001) defined valuable resources as enabling a firm "to conceive or implement strategies that improve its efficiencies and effectiveness." Resources are considered to be rare in the sense that they are not widely available. Barney struggles to define the level of rarity, which is necessary for sustainable competitive advantage. It is possible that rarity becomes less significant if one accepts Penrose's proposition that it is the way in which the resources are used, which is paramount as each firm has the propensity to use a similar resource differently. Barney's final two requirements in relation to resources of imperfectly imitability and substitutability are related. If the resource which is valuable and rare can be imitated by competing firms, then sustained competitive advantage is impossible. Similarly, if the resources or the results of the application of the resources can be achieved through the application of different but strategically equivalent resources, then the competitive advantage cannot be sustained.

Peteraf (1993) proposes a four-factor resource-based model for sustainable competitive advantage, which develops Barney's (2001) four criteria. Peteraf concurs that resources must be heterogeneous if they are to be of value in sustaining competitive advantage. The second factor relates to "ex-post limits to competition" (Peteraf, 1993). This factor includes two of Barney's requirements relating to imitability and substitutability. Clearly, if a competing firm can substitute an alternative resource for the same result, any competitive advantage will be short lived.

However, imitability is more difficult as the basis of the advantage may not be clear or well understood (even by the firm possessing it). The third factor relates to the mobility of the resource. Where the resource is imperfectly mobile, then there is a greater opportunity for sustaining the competitive advantage. A particular case of immobility relates to resources, which have a greater value when used together. The fourth and final factor is that of "ex-ante limits to competition" (Peteraf, 1993).

This proposes that there must have been limited competition for the position now occupied by the firm. If competition had not been limited, then no sustained competitive advantage could have ensued as any potential gain would have been competed away. Like Barney, Peteraf finds that all four factors are required for sustained competitive advantage and that the four factors may, in fact, be related.

Barney (1991) posits that the context of the firm, both in terms of its market positioning and its historical context, are critical factors. Resources which are valuable in one context may have no value in another. The same resource in two different firms could have a significantly different potential as a result of the historical decisions previously taken in each firm and the understanding which might then exist in relation to the possible uses of resources and related outcomes. Like Penrose, Barney appreciates that "for it is managers that are able to understand and describe the economic performance and potential of a firm's endowments. Without such managerial analysis, sustained competitive advantage is not likely" (Barney, 1991).

5.2 Organisational Routines View

In general discussion we all understand the exercise of these skills as routines, which have been learned and improved with practice. More complex decisions can also be the subject of routine behaviour. Many organisations will have an emergency procedure which is to be followed in the event of a fire. Such a procedure will require the evacuation of a building and some basis for ensuring that all employees are accounted for.

Simultaneously, such a procedure might also involve notifying the emergency services and might also involve a trained team of employees tackling the fire in the first instance. Such procedures are often practiced so that if the event actually occurs, the responses and decisions made by individuals will be coherent and safe. This is the essence of a routine.

The literature describes routines in two different ways: as behavioural or cognitive regularities. Behavioural regularities propose routines as "recurrent interaction patterns" (Becker, 2004). These patterns occur in the interaction between a number of actors rather than the actions of one person. To clarify this point, (Dosi et al., 2000) proposed to "reserving the term skill to the individual level and routines to the organisational level." Viewing routines as cognitive regularities would define routines as rules, which suggest how to react to or deal with specific situations. Examples could include standard operating procedures, rules of thumb and programs.

Following Winter (2003) routines are defined as "behaviour that is learned, highly patterned, repetitious, or quasi- repetitious, founded in part in tacit knowledge and the specificity of objectives." Nelson and Winter (2009) stated that well defined routines "structure a large part of organisational functioning at any particular time." Routines develop over time and are based on the history of the organisation (Teece et al., 1997) and also the experience of the individuals involved (Helfat & Peteraf, 2003).

A central premise of the resource-based view is that the resources available to firms are heterogeneous in nature (Barney, 1991). The routines of a firm are a resource and play a critical role in the services which the configuration of resources in any firm can produce. The incremental and context-specific adjustment of a firm's routines is a key source of resource heterogeneity (Helfat & Peteraf, 2003).

Routines allow an organisation to store knowledge. Nelson and Winter (2009) proposed that "the routinisation of activity in an organisation constitutes the most important form of storage of the organisation's specific operational knowledge. Basically, we claim that organisations *remember* by *doing."*

Hilliard and Jacobson (2011) describe the essence of evolutionary theory as "the firm is a repository of knowledge and that knowledge resides in the organisational capabilities that determine the firm's performance." Nelson and Winter (2009) discussed how individuals in organisations respond to the messages they receive, based on their knowledge of the organisation and its requirements rather than being based on the content of the specific message received.

Routines also provide stability and control to organisations. Routines define expected and effectively accepted actions and behaviours in an organisation. Barnard's (1938) description of "a zone of indifference," which "resides in each individual within which orders are acceptable without conscious questions of their authority," echoes the truth described by Nelson and Winter. Kogut and Zander (1992) concur stating that it is the stability in the relationships between capabilities and social knowledge of how the firm operates that "generates the characteristics of inertia in a firm's capabilities." Routines, therefore, allow the organisation to function in a controlled and stable manner, all other things being equal.

All other things do not remain equal indefinitely. The environment in which any firm exists changes over time and may change frequently. As routines are context specific and objective specific, a changing environment may mean that once appropriate routines become obsolete. Negative feedback mechanisms within the routine can be ignored leading to inertia (Becker, 2004). Routines are capable of being changed in response to experience and feedback. This change can be incremental or more fundamental depending on the significance of the changes experienced.

5.3 Organisational Capabilities View

All organisations have capabilities. Citing the example of the airline industry, Dosi et al. (2000), described the ability of an airline to process passengers in a generally uneventful manner from check-in, to boarding, through the flight and safely to the destination. A more in depth view of the delivery of this service reveals a series of organisational routines, which have worked in a harmony of sorts to deliver a maintained aircraft to a specific gate on time, with an appropriately trained crew to operate it, with fuel for the journey and food for the passengers, etc. In this sense, it is easy to understand routines as being building blocks of capabilities (Dosi et al., 2008).

Dosi et al. (2000) attempted to distinguish between routines and capabilities by attributing no "presumption regarding the evident purpose" to routines. This is completely at variance to the definition subsequently used by Winter (2003) and discussed above which firmly places routines in context with a "specificity of objectives" (Winter 2003). The attempted distinction in Dosi et al. (2000) is unnecessary if one considers routines as elements of the construction of capabilities.

Winter (2003) proposes that there are different levels of capability. He defines "zero level" capabilities as the capabilities which allow a firm to function, delivering a consistent rate and quality of production in a market place where the volume and nature of demand are static. Where an organisation changes the product or service being offered, or changes the process by which it is created or changes or adds to the locations where the product or service is offered, then a higher form of organisational capability has been invoked. This distinction is useful as it highlights that all capabilities are not equal, and some capabilities may be completely inadequate in the face of an environment which is changing.

"A distinction can be drawn between technological and organisational capabilities (Dosi et al., 2008). Technological capabilities refer to capabilities, which deal with the physical elements of an organisation's resources. They suggest routines for how to handle such issues and might relate generally, for example, to capabilities in relation to the operation of printing machinery, the control of utilities supplied to a factory, etc. Organisational capabilities relate more to the coordination and social interactions within the organisation and relate more to human relations than the physical resources. There is an overlap between these capabilities as the particular manner in which a physical process may operate might be affected by the human relations context. Equally, the extent of the physical resources available and their condition might influence the interaction taking place. The real value in the distinction is that it is conceivable that very similar technological capabilities could be present in different firms and in quite different contexts, whereas the organisational capabilities are more likely to be heterogeneous among firms as the context and history of each firm will be different.

Bender (2008) introduces an additional typology in describing transformational capabilities as "the enduring ability of an organisation to transform available general knowledge into plant, firm or task specific knowledge and competence" and configurational capabilities as "enduring ability to synthesise novelty by creating new configurations of knowledge, artefacts and actors." Transformational capabilities have a close relationship to the concept of absorptive capacity (Cohen & Levinthal, 1990) which deals with an organisation's ability to assimilate knowledge into to its routines, processes and capabilities.

This typology is supported by Levinthal and March (1993) who describe the need to have capabilities which both explore (pursue new knowledge) and exploit (using and developing things, which are already known). While it is difficult to be prescriptive in relation to a balance between the transformational and configurational efforts, a successful firm will require a balance of both (Bender, 2008).

Helfat and Peteraf (2003) also found that capabilities are subject to lifecycles in a broadly similar way to product or market lifecycles in the marketing literature. This capability lifecycle concept is a useful tool to bring the concepts of resources, path dependency, routines and capabilities together.

The founding stage of the lifecycle requires an organised team with a specific objective which entails the creation of a new capability. The experiences and abilities which the members bring to the team coupled with any other existing resources bring a history and path dependence to the team at its birth. The development stage is where the team is learning and developing its capability in the light of experience.

As the capability development stabilises it enters the maturity stage of the lifecycle where the capability can become more embedded in the organisation through use. Like routines, the exercise of the capability has an impact on how well it is maintained. Once a capability is in maturity, it may be threatened with obsolescence or indeed opportunities for growth or change in some way (Helfat & Peteraf, 2003).

The model proposes that such impacts can lead to one of six possible outcomes: retirement (where the capability is withdrawn by the firm), retrenchment (a decline in the level of the capability), renewal (where the firm searches for and develops new alternatives), replication (where the capability is reproduced in another geographic market), redeployment (where the capability is used in a different but related product market) and finally, recombination (where the capability is combined with another capability or set of capabilities) (Helfat & Peteraf, 2003).

5.4 Dynamic Capabilities View

Teece, Pisano and Shuen (1997) developed an additional perspective on the resource-based view by considering how firms sustain competitive advantage in the face of environmental change, and particularly in environments of considerable change. Teece et al. (1997) stated that a firm must be dynamic, described as "the capacity to renew competences to achieve congruence with the changing business environment" and that it must have capabilities, described as "the role of strategic management in appropriately adapting, integrating and reconfiguring internal and external organisational skills, resources, and functional competences to match the requirements of a changing environment" if it is to sustain competitive advantage.

Eisenhardt and Martin (2000) found that "dynamic capabilities thus are the organisational and strategic routines by which firms achieve new resource configuration as markets emerge, collide, split, evolve and die." These authors argue that as such routines are idiosyncratic to firms but could result in similar outcomes; they cannot, therefore, be the source of sustained competitive advantage. Eisenhardt and Martin found that the processes and routines which would underpin the capability were more in the nature of the best practice than a source of sustained competitive advantage.

Newey and Zahra (2009) held that there was a difference between operating capabilities and dynamic capabilities but that a relationship between them exists. Clearly, dynamic capabilities are likely to change the operating capabilities in organisations as they develop. However, Newey and Zahra (2009) held that "operating capabilities also affect dynamic capabilities by influencing the knowledge that is available for the latter to undertake future reconfigurations of the former." Zahra, Sapienza and Davissson (2006) concur with both the distinction between operational (termed substantive) capabilities and dynamic capabilities and the view that a co-relationship exists between them. Zahra et al. held that this relationship is moderated by organisational knowledge.

Ambrosini, Bowman and Collier (2009) propose three levels of dynamic capabilities, which are related to managers' perceptions of the level of environmental change or dynamism. Incremental dynamic capabilities relate to the incremental changes associated with continuous improvement processes in firms where the environment is effectively stable. Renewing dynamic capabilities relate to a more radical level of change in a substantially more dynamic environment.

Regenerative dynamic capabilities are considered necessary in environments, which are perceived as turbulent by the firm's managers and are the dynamic capability by which the existing dynamic capabilities are changed. If the existing dynamic capabilities are not appropriate to the new environment, then Ambrosini et al. argue that the firm in question may fail. The distinctions in the forms of dynamic capability proposed are useful in that they suggest that not all dynamic capabilities are equal. Echoing the Winters (2003) consideration of zero and first-order capabilities, Ambrosini et al.'s (2009) contribution allows a consideration of dynamic capabilities, which are appropriate in more or less dynamic environments.

Chapter 6:

Classification of Dynamic Capabilities

Wang and Ahmed (2007) identified three higher-order dynamic capabilities, namely absorptive capability, adaptive capability and innovation management capability as the core components of dynamic capability of the firm. Parida et al. (2009) suggested that networking capability could be a part of higher-order dynamic capability constructs. Two other higher-order capabilities: sensing and integrative capabilities were found in the literature (Jusoh & Parnell, 2008; Morgan et al., 2009). In their attempt to review the dynamic capabilities' literature, Eisenhardt (2000) identified seven major component dynamic capabilities, namely product development capabilities, replication capabilities, resource allocation capabilities, coevolving capabilities, knowledge generation capabilities, alliance and acquisition capabilities and exit and jettison capabilities. Many researchers developed constructs to explore six major dynamic capabilities such as *sensing, absorptive, adaptive, innovative, networking and integrative capabilities*.

Isabel Prieto et al. (2009) measured dynamic capabilities as a "multi-dimensional construct" that built on the processes and knowledge associated in the product development. He *et al.* (2006) proposed six first-order dynamic capabilities viz. "customers value creation, technology system, structure system, institutional system, isolation mechanism and drive for change." A number of authors have discussed operations capabilities, technological capabilities and marketing capabilities as key factors for achieving superior innovative performance (Dutta et al., 1999; Kotabe et al., 2002; Krasnikov & Jayachandran, 2008; Wu, 2013; Zhou and Wu, 2010).

The firm capabilities that founded the dynamic capability vary from one industry to another and one firm to anointer based on the firms' resource base. The higher-order dynamic capabilities of the firm majorly build upon firms' capabilities like R&D capability, production capability, marketing capability, etc. The following part of the section discusses innovation management capability of the tissue culture production firms in competitive market conditions.

6.1 Marketing Capability:

Marketing capability indicates the firms' capacity to popularise and market the products with clear understanding on present and future needs of the consumers, approaches to consumer interactions, knowledge on competitors' strategies and approaches. Marketing capabilities are defined as "the integrative processes designed to apply collective knowledge, skills and resources of the firm to market-related needs of the business, enabling the business to add value to its goods and services, adapt to market conditions, take advantage of market opportunities and meet competitive threats" (Vorhies, 1998). Based on the "resource-based based view" and "capacity based view" of the firm (Peteraf, 1993; Teece et al., 1997), marketing researchers stated that "marketing of resources and capabilities can contribute to the creation of a competitive advantage because they may be rare, difficult to achieve, difficult to duplicate and their value can be appropriated by the organization." The ability to gather, disseminate and use market information is a key to the organizational performance and growth (Jaworski & Kohli, 1993).

6.2 Human-Resource Retention Capability:

Human resources are the flesh and backbone of any organization. Hence, maintaining and retaining employees is crucial for effective performance of any organisation. In order to retain talent pool, various strategies are being implemented in both global and domestic organisation regardless of size of the firms. "Retaining the desirable employees is beneficial to an organization in gaining competitive advantage that cannot be substituted by other competitors in terms of producing high morale and satisfied co-workers who will provide better customer service and enhanced productivity, which subsequently resulting in sales generating, customer satisfaction, smooth management succession and improved organizational learning (Heathfield, 2005)." But retaining competent employees more important than recruiting new employees, several employers are underestimated the costs associated with the turnover of efficient and key employees (Ahlrichs, 2000). "Turnover costs can be incurred with issues such as reference checks, security clearance, temporary worker costs, relocation costs, formal training costs and induction expenses (Roodt

& Kotze, 2005). Other invincible costs and hidden costs such as missed deadlines, loss of organizational knowledge, lower morale, and client's negative perception of company image may also take place."

This is why retaining top talent has become a primary concern for many organizations today. Managers have to exert a lot of effort in ensuring the employee's turnover are always low, as they are gaining increasing awareness of which employees are critical to organization since their values to the organization are not easily replicated (Stovel et al., 2002)." Several studies are conducted to know how to seal the turnover of key employees who possessed specific skill and can perform effectively, since the event of skilled employee turnover could lead to low organisational productivity in any industry (Rappaport et al., 2003).

With the realisation of the essence of the employee retention, managers need to consider their employees views on job and satisfaction, working conditions, interpersonal relations with superiors and peers to ensure maintenance and to retain the talent pool in organisations. Further to this, organisations are also needed to maintain good customer relation due to the cohesiveness between employee satisfaction and consumer satisfaction in organisational context (Jolliffe & Farnsworth, 2003).

6.3 Right Sizing capability:

The thrust to enhance the productivity has been high in all these efforts. As a consequence, companies had to find ways to rationalize their manpower to improve productivity and cut their costs quickly. Managers frequently found no options but to reduce the unsuitable and surplus manpower though it had been an emotionally painful process for managers and employees both. Moreover, Burack, E and Singh, R (1995) reveals that government is yet to announce an official Exit Policy. Government-supported exit policy of manpower reduction by 'golden handshake' which were quite successful in government as well as private sectors. Rightsizing implies the organisation ability in determining and maintaining right size of the employment in organisation in order to achieve efficiency and competitive advantage. Implicitly in concept of rightsizing it is assumed that the "company being downsized is essentially over-staffed and that performance levels can be maintained or even improved by reducing the number of the employees." The terms rightsizing is often synonymously used as a euphemism for downsizing. Rightsizing is also commonly called as "reorganizing, re-engineering, restructuring, or downsizing."

In literature, researchers described rightsizing from three different perspectives: First, "as a way of responding quickly to bad economic conditions" which led to more workload, market stagnation and job security issues (Bennett, 1991; Baumohl, 1993); Second, "as a part of their revamping and restructuring business operations strategy" even active and effective organizations proactively rightsized the workforce to achieve competitive advantage (Feldman & Leana, 2002); Third, as a response to external influences (Schuler & Jackson,1987) like laws of land, government regulations, economic slowdown, competition, etc. and as a means to survive their business operation in changing business environment.

6.4 Investment Capability:

Several scholars emphasized the relationship between investment and success of the organisations in achieving competitive edge in changing market conditions (Higgins, 1995). Traditionally, only the investment in R&D activities was being perceived as the key factor for innovation development. However, good number of research studies found that "merely providing heavy investment on R&D activities cannot sustain innovation performance and firm's competitiveness (Yam et al., 2004; Guan & Ma, 2003; Souitaris, 2002; Romijin & Albaladelo, 2002)." In this context, 'Investment capability' is described as the skills and information needed to "identify feasible investment projects; prepare, locate and purchase technologies; staff, design and manage construction; commissioning and start-up."

Lall (1992), viewed investment capability as "skills needed to identify, obtain technology for design, construction and commission of new products/ facilities, determining the capital requirements of the project, the appropriateness of the scale, technology and selected equipment." The spending that firms incurred on different innovation activities show its commitment toward the generation of knowledge that needed for the innovation development. In literature, the several research studies found positive relation between firm's investment in technological innovation and firm performance. It is highlighted in these studies that "investment enables firm to achieve greater capability to meet the demands of its changing domestic and international market (Zahra & George, 2002), thus give the firm a good performance. It also enables a firm to exploit the intangible technological assets, which can be beneficial to the learning process (Xie, 2004)."

6.5 Production Capability:

In literature, production capability is defined as "the firms' ability to integrate, build and reconfigure internal and external production competences to address rapidly changing environments." Organisations are persistently strived to master their firm-specific production prowess, which prevents competitors to spread into their markets. Often, the efficiency of production capability is measured through firms' ability to transform such production capabilities into a source of competitive advantage (Reichstein & Salter, 2006).

In this context, production capability is referred to as "the skills and knowledge required for the operation of the production facilities. Production capability was considered under process, product and industrial engineering functions like debugging and calibration of new equipment, replacing original equipment parts, quality control, reproduction of fixed specifications and designs, accreditation and certification of product quality, design and introduction of new products in-house, operation of the inventory control systems, scheduling production, and monitoring of productivity." High levels of production capability can promote firms to pursue large-scale production through rigorous production process and production cost and high quality of products (Krasnikov & Jayachandran, 2008) and outperform their competitors. Several studies measured the production capability of the firm through the ratio of production cost to total sales (Nair & Filer, 2003).

6.6 Absorptive capacity:

Absorptive capability is the "ability to recognize the value of new information, assimilate it, and apply it to commercial ends (Cohen & Levinthal, 1990)." A particular characteristic of absorptive capacity is the path dependence nature; it induces through generation of new knowledge. Firms' accrued knowledge permits the assimilation and exploitation of new knowledge (Cohen & Levinthal, 1990). Firms that possess valuable knowledge of certain technologies absorb inputs in order to generate outputs in terms of new ideas and products (Tsai, 2001). Lack of this capability is a major barrier to transfer knowledge across subsidiaries and units of a company or among collaborative firms (Szulanski, 1996).

Absorptive capability is a crucial component of firms' dynamic capability; it helps the firm to integrate, build and transform internal and external competencies to business processes to adapt or to create structural changes in markets (Eisenhardt & Martin, 2000). Absorptive capability supports the functioning of operational and other component dynamic capabilities and it reflects the level of dynamic capability of the firm. It is cited in the literature that the organisation exhibits the 'Absorptive capability' the higher it demonstrates the dynamic capability (Woiceshyn & Daellenbach, 2005; Wang & Ahmed, 2007).

6.7 Leadership Capability:

Leadership capability is emerging as a preferred model based on the role of the leader plays in promoting both personal and organizational change, in particular, the role they have in supporting staff to meet and exceed expectations about performance (Callan et al., 2007). In literature, several research studies concluded that leadership can significantly influence the performance of the organisations (Vance & Larson, 2002).

In literature, several studies suggested that leadership capability can be measured through the skills, emotional intelligence, strategic planning ability, co-ordination, influencing, directing, controlling, etc. abilities of leaders in the organisation (Suri Babu et al., 2008). Leadership capability is important because "the success of an organization as a whole depends not on the performance of some remarkable individuals, but on the collective contribution of all members (Jacobs, 1987)."

It is evident that the leadership capability exists at the both individual and collective level in organisation. However, traditionally it has presumed a 'top-down influence' for leadership where the leader is the primary originator and conductor of leadership (Pearce and Conger, 2003; Conger and Riggio, 2012). Leadership is also viewed as a property of the whole organization (O'Connor and Quinn, 2004) where "collective leadership qualities are embedded in the organization's systems and structure (Pasternack et al., 2001)." Pasternack et al. (2001) shared a view that "leadership must not be a solo act performed by a charismatic chief executive officer" and argued that "leadership can be seen as an institutional capacity and a strategic asset."

The leadership capability at an organizational level implies that organizational structure is often intertwined with leadership processes in organizational systems. Organizational structure represents dynamic patterns relationship between organizational members. Organizational leadership capability can be viewed as an "emergent state" or "embedded capacity of the organization" which evolves throughout the life of an organization.

Leadership capabilities are seen as critical to delivering organizational results by O'Regan and Ghobadian (2004) and they say that "as leaders, Chief Executives face an increasingly dynamic, complex and unpredictable environment, technological change, globalization, and changing competitive approaches that impact the overall performance. For organizations to remain competitive, they must maximize the leadership capabilities within the organization."

But the core part of leadership is associated with leaders' skills, knowledge, experience, education, attitude, concern to support followers, concern for organisation development and commitment to pursue organisational objectives as priority beside self-goals (Higgs, 2003).

6.8 Collaboration Capability:

In literature, few research studies found positive relationship between firm's strategic alliances and firm performance (Shan et al., 1994). In contrast this, Deeds and Hill (1996) found negative relationship between alliances and firm performance in case of new and high-technology ventures due to diminishing of marginal returns with an increase in the number of alliances.

It also observed that one of the reasons for an inverted U-shaped relationship in collaborating firms is that formation of the most productive alliances at first and subsequent weaker alliance formation in later period and led to the networking overload (Zahra et al., 2000). Transaction costs among the collaborating firms rises as firms enter more alliances and beyond certain point possible gains from the addition of new alliance outweighed by the associated transaction costs (Jones and Hill, 1988).

In literature, this capability was studied by assessing the inflection points of the firm at which any further collaboration with another firm can show a negative effect on overall performance of the firm. Hence, such inflection point represents the maximum level of firms' productive alliancing capability; several studies measured the organisational collaboration capabilities by calculating those inflection points (Godfrey and Hill, 1995). Browning et al. (1995) studied the negative effects of coordination in "SEMA TECH" consortium and found that "high level of confusion and ambiguity about roles and responsibilities" are attributed to the negative effects observed in the study.

Anand and Khanna (2000) and Lambe et al. (2002) found the positive effect of 'alliance experience' on firm performance. They argued that "firms with considerable alliance experience know how to deal with the interpersonal relations at the inter-organizational level. It involves tacit knowledge and develops over time."

Skilful managers are capable of establish effective communication and to stimulate joint sense making (Luo, 2007). Furthermore, appropriate and timely sharing of information acts as a bonding mechanism which facilitates the realization of mutual benefits by reducing misunderstandings (Sarkar et al., 2001) resolving disputes, aligning perceptions and expectations (Aulakh et al., 1996; Luo, 2001), and specifying clear roles (Sivadas & Dwyer, 2000). Hence, monitoring based on interpersonal interactions will help to build trust (Aulakh et al., 1996).

Finally, a firm's partner identity propensity contributes to the extent to which it can attract partners with congruent organizational cultures and capabilities that reduces a relational risk (Das & Teng, 2001a). Without this ability, the firm may choose a socially incompatible partner, which hinders a harmonious alliance relationship and negatively influences collaborative effectiveness because incompatible partners face higher levels of stress when they attempt to blend their values, norms, capabilities, and organizational cultures (Das & Teng, 2001b; Sarkar et al., 2001). These differences hinder role socialization (Smith & Barclay, 1997), which makes it more difficult in turn for the interfacing managers to work together (Sarkar et al., 2001).

Deeds and Hill (1996) hypothesized that the firm's collaborations show an influence on firm's innovative potential. However, he could not find any support for this hypothesis in his studies. This finding led to the postulation of another hypothesis that firms tend to undermine their innovative potentials once they exceed a certain number of alliances. It led to the further grounding for the existence of trade-offs between cooperation and innovative potential.

However, there is no strong empirical evidence observed to support that collaborations improve firm's innovativeness (de Man & Duysters, 2005). This stream of literature argues that cooperation may be enhancing innovativeness up to a point, but this effect can be reversed as firms engage in an increasing number of cooperative agreements (Deeds & Hill, 1996; Deeds, 2001). This negative effect set in as engaging in an increasing number of cooperative agreements puts strains on firms' capabilities to coordinate an increasing number of such agreements (Gulati & Singh, 1998).

Contrary to above expectations, another stream of this literature argues that "engagement in an increasing number of cooperative agreements allows firms to accumulate experience over time in the management and coordination of cooperative agreements (Zollo et al., 2002b; Lazaric & Marengo, 2000).

At the same time firms with a longer experience in cooperation have greater innovative potentials than firms with less experience in cooperation (Hoang & Rothaermel, 2005)." It suggests that firms become better in managing their collaboration and overcome coordination failures by continuous learning over time. Recent research also found that specific mechanisms that built through accumulated experiences to manage agreements accelerated the returns of alliances (Heimeriks & Duysters, 2007). Therefore, it is suggested to assess firm's alliance management capability by the number of alliances, which are being productively managed in a simultaneous fashion.

Chapter 7:
Innovation Management Capability

Innovation is the major source for competitive advantage and superior performance of any business organisation (Hult et al., 2004). According to Keizer et al. (2002) innovation enables the small and medium-sized enterprises (SMEs) to contribute to the vital economic performance of any industry. In order to survive increasing competition, organisations must effectively leverage their capabilities for innovation management (Vertinsky, 2003). Developing and deploying innovation management capability have to be implemented as a higher-order dynamic capability of organisation (Papadopoulos and Karagouni, 2007).

Firms by deploying their capabilities and resources for the development of dynamic capability can sustain a competitive advantage (Teece, 2009). Fan (2006) argued that just by improving their internal competency in doing R&D does not result in building higher-order capabilities; firms need to leverage internal and external resources with continuous learning to build such higher-order dynamic capabilities.

Innovation management capability as a new field of study is attracting interest of several scholars (Forsman, 2011). Innovation management capability is defined as "a comprehensive set of characteristics of a firm that facilities and supports its strategies in innovation development and in appropriating the benefits/returns of innovation for sustainable competitive advantage" (Burgelman et al., 2004). Therefore, it involves "multi-dimensional, complex, interactive innovation activities with resource re-deployment in order to gain competitive advantage" (Wang et al., 2008; Chiesa et al., 1996).

In literature, several scholars quoted innovation management as a higher-order dynamic capability (Perdomo-Ortiz et al., 2006) i.e. "a learned and stable pattern of collective activity through which the organization systematically generates and modifies its operating routines and capabilities in pursuit of improved effectiveness" (Zollo & Winter, 2002a). According to Dodgson and Bessant (1996), innovation management capability is the key feature of firms, which enable them to define and develop competences to create competitive advantage. Vertinsky (2003) concluded that intensifying innovation efforts that expand firms' product offering or market reach and/or increased the emphasis placed on innovation and in-house R&D facilitated the development of radical products.

In this context, innovation management capability is understood as it built upon the firm's capabilities like technological learning and development capabilities, operational capabilities, transaction capabilities and management capabilities. Organisations always strive to integrate these capabilities to promote innovation for achieving competitive advantage in the market. Badawy (2011) described that the importance of the successful innovation management is to focus on the innovation process, the technology development and the utilization of technology in both business and industry.

Innovation management capability helps the organisation to choose right technologies and strategic use of such technologies (Rush et al., 2007); to develop new products, services, techniques and methods (Afuah, 2002; Zhou & Wu, 2010). Innovation management capability can be achieved by changing the production function to internalise the new knowledge to produce technological change and, consequently, new processes and products through effective learning processes (Lall, 1992). These learning processes involve "acquisition, imitation, adaptation, modification and/or the development of a new set of knowledge and technical systems for internal use." As a result of this process, new goods and services could be produced with high technical standards.

Yam et al. (2004) described that "technological innovation capability constitutes seven component capabilities namely 1. *Learning capability* is the capacity to identify, assimilate, and exploit existing knowledge and competence essential for a firm's competitive success. 2. *R&D capability* refers to a firm's ability to integrate R&D strategy, project implementation, product portfolio management and R&D expenditure. 3. *Resource allocation capability* is the firm's ability to mobilize and expand its technological, human and financial resources in the innovation process. 4. *Manufacturing capability* refers to the ability to transform R&D results into products, which meet market needs, in accordance with design request and can also be manufactured in batches. 5. *Marketing capability* indicates the capacity to publicize and sell the products based on understanding consumer's current and future needs, customer's access approaches, and competitors' knowledge. 6. *Organizing capability* is the capacity to constitute a well-established organizational structure, cultivate organizational culture, coordinate the work of all activities towards shared objectives, and influence the speed of innovational processes through the infrastructure it creates for developmental projects. 7. *Strategic planning capability* is the capacity to identify internal strengths and weaknesses and external opportunities and threats, adopt different types of strategies that can adapt to environment changes for the excelling in the highly competitive environment."

Firm's competitive edge changes with shifts in "exogenous factors: acquisitions and collaborations" and "endogenous factors: R&D expenditure and manpower" (Sher & Yang, 2005). It is being considered R&D spending as one of the most important factors for new-product development (Sanuri Mohd Mokhtar, 2013) even though the number of organizations preferred to outsource their R&D functions (Calantone & Stanko, 2007; Chiesa and Toletti, 2004). However, Agndal and Nordin (2009) argue that if R&D activities are outsourced then the deep knowledge about the product may be lost. The dynamic nature markets rendered each firm to engage in continuous or periodic innovation development and reorientation (Tamayo-Torres et al., 2010).

Chapter 8:

Summary

Business organisations are increasingly under pressure to sustain their competitive advantage in present rapid technological changes, globalised markets, and blurring of industry boundaries particularly through the proliferation of open networks and new technologies. Since innovation can be crucial for the growth and success of a firm (Andrews & Smith, 1996; Sethi et al., 2001), studies of innovation have taken many different research directions in numerous management fields (see Hoffman et al., 1998). Wolfe (1994) described innovation literature as a "fragmented corpus" and scholars from diverse backgrounds adopted different "ontological" and "epistemological" positions to investigate and report the innovation phenomenon which is very complex and multidimensional.

Drucker (1994) argues that innovation management knowledge is the only way to convert change into opportunities. Firms which possess a higher level of innovation management capability tend to have a higher chance of becoming successful in their businesses compared to their peers, as they are more capable of dealing with the complexity of the innovation process (Tidd et al., 1997).

Systematic literature review was undertaken in order to develop conceptual framework and achieve research aim and objectives. As noted before, this study draws on four main theories (resource-based view, organisational routines view, organisational capabilities view and dynamic capabilities view) for examining the impact of organisational first-order capabilities on higher-order innovation management capability. The resource-based theory of the firm underpins the notion of capabilities for a firm's innovative functions.

The resource-based theory focuses on a bundle of resources and capabilities that are heterogeneous, scarce, durable, not easily traded and difficult to imitate as sources for the development of sustainable competitive advantage (Penrose, 1959; Wernerfelt, 1984; Barney, 1991; Peteraf, 1993, Eng & Okten, 2011). Possessing diversified resources cannot guarantee the competitive advantage and it requires skilful actions, which use and blend the resource base of the organisations.

Nelson and Winter used the term 'Organisational Routines to refer such skilful activities needed for the effective utilization of organisational resources to develop a competitive advantage. Organisational routines are regular and predictable patterns of activity, which are made up of a sequence of coordinated actions by individuals. Routines develop over time and are based on the history of the organisation (Teece et al., 1997, Nelson & Winter, 2009) and also the experience of the individuals involved (Levinthal & March, 1993, Helfat & Peteraf, 2003). The routines of a firm are a resource and play a critical role in the services which the configuration of resources in any firm can produce.

The incremental and context-specific adjustment of a firm's routines is a key source of resource heterogeneity (Helfat & Peteraf, 2003). According to Hilliard (2004), routines allow an organisation to store knowledge. Nelson & Winter (2009) propose that "the routinisation of activity in an organisation constitutes the most important form of storage of the organisation's specific operational knowledge."

The environment in which any firm exists changes over time and may change frequently. As routines are context specific and objective specific, a changing environment may mean that once appropriate routines become obsolete. Helfat and Peteraf (2003) define organisational capabilities as the ability of an organisation to "perform a set of coordinated tasks, utilising organisational resources, for the purpose of achieving a particular end result". This focus on a defined result is generally accepted in the literature (Winter, 2003, Dosi et al., 2008).

Helfat and Peteraf (2003) also found that capabilities are subject to lifecycles in a broadly similar way to product or market lifecycles in the marketing literature. This capability lifecycle concept is a useful tool to bring the concepts of resources, path dependency, routines and capabilities together to develop a new perspective of competitive advantage, i.e. dynamic capabilities of the organisations.

Dynamic capabilities are a set of unique and recognizable processes in organisations such as product development, strategic decision making, networking, etc. and are neither vague nor tautological. Fan et al.

(2009) summarized the aspects of dynamic capabilities as the competencies that allow a firm to quickly reconfigure its organizational structure and routines in response to new opportunities. They discussed the dynamic capabilities that are related with cost reduction, outsourcing, knowledge networking and knowledge management.

Tony Davila et al. (2012) classified dynamic capability in to "Financial Management Capability, Product Development Capability, Human Resource Management Capability, Strategic Planning Capability, Sales and Marketing Capability, Partnership Management Capability." Ho *et al.* (2011) examined the influence of technological capabilities and design capabilities on technology commercialization and observed that both technological and design capabilities have positive influence on technology commercialization.

It is found that, dynamic capabilities are also context specific and vary across the industry. Based on the resources and capabilities, firms build different dynamic capabilities to sustain their business in changing conditions. Wang and Ahmed (2007) identified three higher-order dynamic capabilities, namely absorptive capability, adaptive capability and innovation management capability as the core components of dynamic capabilities. Parida (2008) considered to include networking capability as a part of higher-order dynamic capability constructs. Two other higher-order capabilities: sensing and integrative capabilities were found in the literature (Morgan et al., 2009).

In their attempt to review the dynamic capabilities' literature, Eisenhardt and Martin (2000) identified seven major first-order dynamic capabilities, namely product development capabilities, replication capabilities, resource allocation capabilities, coevolving capabilities, knowledge generation capabilities, alliance and acquisition capabilities and exit and jettison capabilities. Several researchers have also developed constructs to explore six major higher-order dynamic capabilities such as *sensing, absorptive, adaptive, innovative, networking and integrative capabilities*. Papadopoulos and Karagouni (2007) stated that innovation management capability has to be developed and deployed as higher-order dynamic capability.

Innovation management capability is a source of competitiveness for any firm. Innovation Management is a higher-order dynamic capability (Perdomo-Ortiz et al., 2006), i.e. "a learned and stable pattern of collective activity through which the organization systematically generates and modifies its operating routines and capabilities in pursuit of improved effectiveness" (Zollo & Winter, 2002b). According to Dodgson and Bessant (1996), innovation management capability is the key feature of firms, which enable them to define and develop competences to create competitive advantage. In order to sustain the intense competition, organizations are needed to leverage their capabilities effectively (Vertinsky, 2003). Indeed, only firms which are able to deploy their resources and capabilities upon the dynamic capability framework can create and sustain a competitive advantage (Teece, 2009).

Innovation management capability has been defined as a comprehensive set of characteristics of a firm that facilities and supports its strategies in innovation development and in appropriating the benefits of such innovation for attaining the competitive advantage in the market (Burgelman et al., 2004). The innovation management capability is understood as both the technological learning process which translates resources into the technology and operation capabilities which appropriates the returns of innovation, as well as the managerial and transactional routines represented by the management and transaction capabilities. Badawy (2010) described that the importance of the successful innovation management is to focus on the innovation process, the technology development and the utilization of technology in both business and industry.

BIBLIOGRAPHY:

Afuah, A. (2002). Mapping technological capabilities into product markets and competitive advantage: the case of cholesterol drugs. *Strategic Management Journal*, 23(2), 171-179.

Abelson, M. A., & Baysinger, B. D. (1984). Optimal and dysfunctional turnover: Toward an organizational level model. *Academy of management Review*, 9(2), 331-341.

ABLE-BioSpectrum (2014). The Twelth Survery of Indian Biotech Industry, Volume 12(1).

Agndal, H., & Nordin, F. (2009). Consequences of outsourcing for organizational capabilities: some experiences from best practice. *Benchmarking: An International Journal*, 16(3), 316-334.

Ahlrichs, N. S. (2000). *Competing for talent: Key recruitment and retention strategies for becoming an employer of choice*. Davies-Black Pub..

Akamavi, R. K. (2005). A research agenda for investigation of product innovation in the financial services sector. *Journal of Services Marketing*,19(6), 359-378.

Akintayo, D. (2012). Working environment, workers' morale and perceived productivity in industrial organizations in Nigeria. *Education Research Journal*,2(3), 87-93.

Alexander, J. A., Bloom, J. R., &Nuchols, B. A. (1994). Nursing turnover and hospital efficiency: an organization-level analysis. Industrial Relations: A Journal of Economy and society, 33(4), 505-520

Ambrosini, V., Bowman, C., & Collier, N. (2009). Dynamic capabilities: an exploration of how firms renew their resource base. *British Journal of Management*, 20(s1), S9-S24.

Anand, B. N., & Khanna, T. (2000). Do firms learn to create value? The case of alliances. *Strategic management journal*, 21(3), 295-315.

Andrews, J., & Smith, D. C. (1996). In search of the marketing imagination: Factors affecting the creativity of marketing programs for mature products.*Journal of Marketing Research*, 174-187.

Arditti, J. (2011). Conservation News Conservation through Propagation.*Orchids, 80* (2), 114.

Argote, L., Ingram, P., Levine, J. M., & Moreland, R. L. (2000). Knowledge transfer in organizations: Learning from the experience of others. *Organizational behavior and human decision processes*, 82(1), 1-8.

Aulakh, P. S., Kotabe, M., & Sahay, A. (1996). Trust and performance in cross-border marketing partnerships: A behavioral approach. *Journal of international business studies*, 1005-1032.

Avermaete, T., Viaene, J., Morgan, E. J., & Crawford, N. (2003).Determinants of innovation in small food firms. *European Journal of Innovation Management*,6(1), 8-17.

Babajide, E. O. (2000). Comparative study of male and female leadership style in banking industry. *Unpublished Ph. D. Thesis, University of Ibadan, Ibadan*.

Badawy, M. K. (2011). Is open innovation a field of study or a communication barrier to theory development?: A perspective. *Technovation*, 31(1), 65-67.

Barkema, H. G., Baum, J. A., &Mannix, E. A. (2002). Management challenges in a new time. *Academy of Management Journal*, 45(5), 916-930.

Barnard, C. I. (1938). The theory of authority. *The functions of the executive*.

Barney, J. (1991). Firm resources and sustained competitive advantage.*Journal of management*, 17(1), 99-120.

Barney, J. B. (2001). Resource-based theories of competitive advantage: A ten-year retrospective on the resource-based view. *Journal of management*,27(6), 643-650.

Baumohl, B. (1993). When downsizing becomes dumbsizing. *Time (March 15)*,55.
Becker, M. C. (2004). Organizational routines: a review of the literature.*Industrial and corporate change, 13*(4), 643-678.
Bender, G. (2008). How to Grasp Innovativeness of Organizations: outline of a conceptual tool. *Innovation in Low-Tech Firms and Industries. Cheltenham, Northampton, Edward Elgar*, 25-42.
Bennett, A. (1991). Downsizing doesn't necessarily bring an upswing in corporate profitability. *Wall Street Journal*, 6.
Bergmann, L. (1960). Growth and division of single cells of higher plants in vitro.*The Journal of general physiology, 43*(4), 841-851.
Bethel, J. E., & Liebeskind, J. (1993). The effects of ownership structure on corporate restructuring. *Strategic Management Journal, 14*(S1), 15-31.
Bougrain, F., & Haudeville, B. (2002).Innovation, collaboration and SMEs internal research capacities. *Research policy, 31*(5), 735-747.
Brainard, W. C., & Tobin, J. (1968). Pitfalls in financial model building. *The American Economic Review*, 99-122.
Brewin, D. G., Monchuk, D. C., & Partridge, M. D. (2009).Examining the adoption of product and process innovations in the Canadian food processing industry. *Canadian Journal of Agricultural Economics/Revue canadienned'agroeconomie, 57*(1), 75-97.
Brown, C., & Medoff, J. (1978).Trade unions in the production process. *The Journal of Political Economy*, 355-378.
Brown, S. L., & Eisenhardt, K. M. (1998). *Competing on the edge: Strategy as structured chaos.* Harvard Business Press.
Browning, L. D., Beyer, J. M., &Shetler, J. C. (1995).Building cooperation in a competitive industry: SEMATECH and the semiconductor industry. *Academy of Management Journal, 38*(1), 113-151.
Buck, J. M., & Watson, J. L. (2002). Retaining staff employees: The relationship between human resources management strategies and organizational commitment. *Innovative Higher Education, 26*(3), 175-193.
Bunse, K., Vodicka, M., Schönsleben, P., Brülhart, M., & Ernst, F. O. (2011).Integrating energy efficiency performance in production management–gap analysis between industrial needs and scientific literature. *Journal of Cleaner Production, 19*(6), 667-679.
Burack, E and Singh, R (1995) 'The New Employment Relations Compact' Human Resource Planning Vol 18 No 1 pp 12-19
Burgelman, R. A., & Sayles, L. R. (2004).Transforming invention into innovation: the conceptualization stage. *Strategic Management of Technology and Innovation. McGraw-Hill, Boston*, 682-690.
Calantone, R. J., & Stanko, M. A. (2007). Drivers of Outsourced Innovation: An Exploratory Study. *Journal of Product Innovation Management, 24*(3), 230-241.
Callan, V., Mitchell, J., Clayton, B., & Smith, L. (2007).Approaches for sustaining and building management and leadership capability in vocational education.
Caplin, S. M., & Steward, F. C. (1948). Effect of coconut milk on the growth of explants from carrot root. *Science, 108*(2815), 655-657.
Carlson, P. S. (Ed.). (2013). *The biology of crop productivity.* Elsevier.
Cascio, W. F., & Young, C. E. (2003).Financial consequences of employment-change decisions in major US corporations, 1982-2000. *Resizing the organization*, 131-156.
Cascio, W. F., Young, C. E., & Morris, J. R. (1997).Financial consequences of employment-change decisions in major US corporations. *Academy of management Journal, 40*(5), 1175-1189.

Cebon, P., Newton, P., & Noble, P. (1999). Innovation in firms: towards a framework for indicator development. *Melbourne Business School, Working Paper*, (99-9).

Chiesa, V., Coughlan, P., & Voss, C. A. (1996). Development of a technical innovation audit. *Journal of product innovation management, 13*(2), 105-136.

Chiesa, V., & Toletti, G. (2004). Network of Collaborations for Innovation: The Case of Biotechnology. *Technology analysis and strategic management,16*(1), 73-96.

Cinches, M. F. C. (2012). Organizational Retention Capability Models: The Case of Autonomous Universities in Southern Philippines. *Liceo Journal of Higher Education Research, 8*(1).

Clarysse, B., &Bruneel, J. (2007). Nurturing and growing innovative start-ups: the role of policy as integrator. R&d Management, 37(2), 139-149.

Cockburn, I. M., & Henderson, R. M. (1998).Absorptive capacity, coauthoring behavior, and the organization of research in drug discovery. *The Journal of Industrial Economics, 46*(2), 157-182.

Cohen, W. M., & Levinthal, D. A. (1990). Absorptive capacity: a new perspective on learning and innovation. *Administrative science quarterly*, 128-152.

Coleman, M. (2007). Gender and educational leadership in England: A comparison of secondary headteachers' views over time. *School Leadership and Management, 27*(4), 383-399.

Conant, J. S., Mokwa, M. P., &Varadarajan, P. R. (1990). Strategic types, distinctive marketing competencies and organizational performance: a multiple measures-based study. Strategic management journal, 11(5), 365-383.

Conger, J. A., & Riggio, R. E. (2012). *The practice of leadership: Developing the next generation of leaders*. John Wiley & Sons.

Cooper, W. W., Seiford, L. M., & Zhu, J. (2000). A unified additive model approach for evaluating inefficiency and congestion with associated measures in DEA. *Socio-Economic Planning Sciences, 34*(1), 1-25.

Damanpour, F., & Gopalakrishnan, S. (1998). Theories of organizational structure and innovation adoption: the role of environmental change. *Journal of Engineering and Technology Management, 15*(1), 1-24.

Danneels, E., & Kleinschmidtb, E. J. (2001). Product innovativeness from the firm's perspective: its dimensions and their relation with project selection and performance. *Journal of Product Innovation Management, 18*(6), 357-373.

Das, T. K., &Teng, B. S. (2001a). Trust, control, and risk in strategic alliances: An integrated framework. *Organization studies, 22*(2), 251-283.

Das, T. K., &Teng, B. S. (2001b).A risk perception model of alliance structuring. *Journal of International Management, 7*(1), 1-29.

Davila, T., Epstein, M., & Shelton, R. (2012). *Making innovation work: How to manage it, measure it, and profit from it*. FT Press.

De Man, A. P., & Duysters, G. (2005). Collaboration and innovation: a review of the effects of mergers, acquisitions and alliances on innovation. *Technovation,25*(12), 1377-1387.

De Meuse, K. P., Bergmann, T. J., Vanderheiden, P. A., & Roraff, C. E. (2004). New evidence regarding organizational downsizing and a firm's financial performance: A long-term analysis. *Journal of Managerial Issues*, 155-177.

Deeds, D. L. (2001).The role of R&D intensity, technical development and absorptive capacity in creating entrepreneurial wealth in high technology start-ups. *Journal of Engineering and Technology Management, 18*(1), 29-47.

Deeds, D. L., & Hill, C. W. (1996). Strategic alliances and the rate of new product development: an empirical study of entrepreneurial biotechnology firms.*Journal of Business Venturing, 11*(1), 41-55.

De Long, J. B. (1998). Estimating world GDP, one million BC–present. *Website document at http://econ161. berkeley. edu/ TCEH/ 2000/ World_GDP/ Estimating_World_GDP. htm.*

Dodgson, M., & Bessant, J. R. (1996).Effective innovation policy.
Dodgson, M., &Hinze, S. (2000). Indicators used to measure the innovation process: defects and possible remedies. *Research Evaluation, 9*(2), 101-114.
Dosi, G., Faillo, M., & Marengo, L. (2008). Organizational capabilities, patterns of knowledge accumulation and governance structures in business firms: an introduction. *Organization Studies, 29*(8-9), 1165-1185.
Dosi, G., Nelson, R. R., & Winter, S. G. (2000). Introduction: The nature and dynamics of organizational capabilities. *The nature and dynamics of organizational capabilities, 1*, 24.
Drucker, P. F., & Drucker, P. F. (1994). *Post-capitalist society*.Routledge.
Dutta, S., Narasimhan, O., & Rajiv, S. (1999). Success in high-technology markets: Is marketing capability critical?. *Marketing Science, 18*(4), 547-568.
Dutta, S., Narasimhan, O. M., & Rajiv, S. (2005). Conceptualizing and measuring capabilities: Methodology and empirical application. *Strategic Management Journal, 26*(3), 277-285.
Easterby-Smith, M., Thorpe, R., & Jackson, P. (2012). *Management research*.Sage.
Eisenhardt, K. M., & Martin, J. A. (2000). Dynamic capabilities: what are they?.*Strategic management journal, 21*(10-11), 1105-1121.
Eng, T. Y., & Okten, D. (2011). Exploring a dynamic framework of innovative capability: a theoretical integration of technological and marketing capabilities.*Technology Analysis & Strategic Management, 23*(9), 1001-1013.
Erdil, S., Erdil, O., & Keskin, H. (2004).The relationships between market orientation, firm innovativeness and innovation performance. *Journal of Global Business and Technology, 1*(1), 1-11.
Erickson, T., & Whited, T. M. (2006). On the accuracy of different measures of q. *Financial management, 35*(3), 5-33.
Fan, P. (2006).Catching up through developing innovation capability: evidence from China's telecom-equipment industry. *Technovation, 26*(3), 359-368.
Fan, Z. P., Feng, B., Sun, Y. H., &Ou, W. (2009).Evaluating knowledge management capability of organizations: a fuzzy linguistic method. *Expert Systems with Applications, 36*(2), 3346-3354.
Farrell, M. A., & Mavondo, F. (2005). The effect of downsizing-redesign strategies on business performance: Evidence from Australia. *Asia Pacific Journal of Human Resources, 43*(1), 98-116.
Feldman, D. C., Leana, C. R., &Bolino, M. C. (2002). Underemployment and relative deprivation among re-employed executives. Journal of Occupational and Organizational Psychology, 75(4), 453-471.
Filatotchev, I., Buck, T., & Zhukov, V. (2000). Downsizing in privatized firms in Russia, Ukraine, and Belarus. *Academy of Management Journal, 43*(3), 286-304.
Forsman, H. (2011). Innovation capacity and innovation development in small enterprises. A comparison between the manufacturing and service sectors.*Research Policy, 40*(5), 739-750.
Francis, D., & Bessant, J. (2005).Targeting innovation and implications for capability development. *Technovation, 25*(3), 171-183.
Fredrickson, J. W. (1984). The comprehensiveness of strategic decision processes: Extension, observations, future directions. *Academy of Management Journal, 27*(3), 445-466.
Freeman, S. J., & Cameron, K. S. (1993). Organizational downsizing: A convergence and reorientation framework. *Organization Science, 4*(1), 10-29.
Fuchs, P. H., Mifflin, K. E., Miller, D., & Whitney, J. O. (2000). Strategic integration: Competing in the age of capabilities. *California Management Review, 42*(3), 118-147.

Garcia, R., & Calantone, R. (2002). A critical look at technological innovation typology and innovativeness terminology: a literature review. *Journal of product innovation management*, *19*(2), 110-132.

Garg, V. K., Walters, B. A., & Priem, R. L. (2003). Chief executive scanning emphases, environmental dynamism, and manufacturing firm performance.*Strategic management journal*, *24*(8), 725-744.

Gautheret, R. J. (1939). Sur la possibilité de réaliser la culture indéfinie des tissus de tubercules de carotte. *CR Acad. Sci*, *208*, 118-120.

Ghiselli, E. E. (1971). Explorations in managerial talent.

Ghobadian, A., & O'Regan, N. (2006).The impact of ownership on small firm behaviour and performance. *International Small Business Journal*, *24*(6), 555-586.

Godfrey, P. C., & Hill, C. W. (1995).The problem of unobservables in strategic management research. *Strategic management journal*, *16*(7), 519-533.

Greve, H. R. (2003). A behavioral theory of R&D expenditures and innovations: Evidence from shipbuilding. *Academy of Management Journal*, *46*(6), 685-702.

Guan, J., & Ma, N. (2003). Innovative capability and export performance of Chinese firms. *Technovation*, *23*(9), 737-747.

Guedj, I., Huang, J. C., & Sulaeman, J. (2009).Internal capital allocation and firm performance. *Available at SSRN 1327797*.

Gulati, R., & Singh, H. (1998). The architecture of cooperation: Managing coordination costs and appropriation concerns in strategic alliances.*Administrative science quarterly*, 781-814.

Gunday, G., Ulusoy, G., Kilic, K., & Alpkan, L. (2011).Effects of innovation types on firm performance. *International Journal of Production Economics*,*133*(2), 662-676.

Gutek, B. A., Searle, S., & Klepa, L. (1991). Rational versus gender role explanations for work-family conflict. *Journal of applied psychology*, *76* (4), 560.

Haberlandt G. 1902. KultuversuchemitisoliertenPflanzenzellen. *Sitzugsberichte der Academie der Wissenschafte Wien,Mathematische und Naturwissenschaften Klasse Abhandlungen*111: 69–92.

Harrigan, K. R. (1985). Vertical integration and corporate strategy. *Academy of Management journal*, *28*(2), 397-425.

Hayward, M. L. (2002). When do firms learn from their acquisition experience? Evidence from 1990 to 1995. *Strategic Management Journal*, *23*(1), 21-39.

He, X., Li, X., & Fang, H. (2006). Measuring and efficiency of dynamic capabilities: an empirical study in China (Chin). *Management World*, *3*, 94-103.

Heathfield, S. M. (2005). Top Ten Ways to Retain Your Great Employees.*About Human Resources, About Inc*.

Heimeriks, K. H., & Duysters, G. (2007). Alliance capability as a mediator between experience and alliance performance: an empirical investigation into the alliance capability development process. *Journal of Management Studies*,*44*(1), 25-49.

Helfat, C. E., Finkelstein, S., Mitchell, W., Peteraf, M., Singh, H., Teece, D., & Winter, S. G. (2009). *Dynamic capabilities: Understanding strategic change in organizations*. John Wiley & Sons.

Helfat, C., & Peteraf, M. (2009). Understanding dynamic capabilities: progress along a developmental path. *Strategic organization*, *7*(1), 91.

Henderson, R. M., & Clark, K. B. (1990). Architectural innovation: The reconfiguration of existing product technologies and the failure of established firms. *Administrative science quarterly*, 9-30.

Henderson, R., & Cockburn, I. (1994). Measuring competence? Exploring firm effects in pharmaceutical research. *Strategic management journal*, *15*(S1), 63-84.

Higgins, J. M. (1995). Innovation: the core competence. *Planning review*, *23*(6), 32-36.

Higgs, M. (2003). How can we make sense of leadership in the 21st century?.*Leadership & organization development journal, 24*(5), 273-284.

Hilliard, R. (2004, May). Tacit Knowledge and Dynamic Capability: The Importance of Penrosian 'Image'. In *DRUID Summer Conference in Elsinore, June, Denmark.*

Hilliard, R., & Jacobson, D. (2011). Cluster versus firm-specific factors in the development of dynamic capabilities in the pharmaceutical industry in Ireland: A study of responses to changes in environmental protection regulations.*Regional Studies, 45*(10), 1319-1328.

Ho, Y. C., Fang, H. C., & Lin, J. F. (2011). Technological and design capabilities: is ambidexterity possible?. *Management Decision, 49*(2), 208-225.

Hoang, H. A., & Rothaermel, F. T. (2010). Leveraging internal and external experience: exploration, exploitation, and R&D project performance. *Strategic Management Journal, 31*(7), 734-758.

Hoang, H., &Rothaermel, F. T. (2005).The effect of general and partner-specific alliance experience on joint R&D project performance. *Academy of Management Journal, 48*(2), 332-345.

Hoffman, K., Parejo, M., Bessant, J., &Perren, L. (1998). Small firms, R&D, technology and innovation in the UK: a literature review. *Technovation, 18*(1), 39-55.

Hooley, G. J., Greenley, G. E., Cadogan, J. W., &Fahy, J. (2005). The performance impact of marketing resources. *Journal of Business Research,58*(1), 18-27.

Hult, G. T. M., Hurley, R. F., & Knight, G. A. (2004). Innovativeness: Its antecedents and impact on business performance. *Industrial marketing management, 33*(5), 429-438.

Iansiti, M. (2000). How the incumbent can win: managing technological transitions in the semiconductor industry. *Management Science, 46*(2), 169-185.

IBISWorld Industry Report: Global Biotechnology, July 2014. www.ibisworld.com

Jacobs, T. O., & Jaques, E. (1987).Leadership in complex systems. *Human productivity enhancement, 2,* 7-65.

James, L., & Mathew, L. (2012). Employee Retention Strategies. *JOURNAL OF INDIAN MANAGEMENT,* 79.

Jaworski, B. J., & Kohli, A. K. (1993). Market orientation: antecedents and consequences. *The Journal of marketing,* 53-70.

Jolliffe, L., & Farnsworth, R. (2003). Seasonality in tourism employment: human resource challenges. *International Journal of Contemporary Hospitality Management, 15*(6), 312-316.

Jones, G. R., & Hill, C. W. (1988). Transaction cost analysis of strategy-structure choice. Strategic management journal, 9(2), 159-172.

Ju, M., Fung, H. G., & Mano, H. (2013). Firm Capabilities and Performance.*Chinese economy, 46*(5), 86-104.

Jusoh, R., & Parnell, J. A. (2008). Competitive strategy and performance measurement in the Malaysian context: An exploratory study. *Management Decision, 46*(1), 5-31.

Kacmar, K. M., Andrews, M. C., Van Rooy, D. L., Steilberg, R. C., &Cerrone, S. (2006). Sure everyone can be replaced… but at what cost? Turnover as a predictor of unit-level performance. *Academy of Management journal, 49*(1), 133-144.

Kanter, R. M. (1999). From spare change to real change: The social sector as beta site for business innovation. *Harvard business review, 77,* 122-133.

Kazozcu, S. B. (2011). Role of strategic flexibility in the choice of turnaround strategies: A resource based approach. *Procedia-Social and Behavioral Sciences, 24,* 444-459.

Keizer, J. A., Dijkstra, L., &Halman, J. I. (2002). Explaining innovative efforts of SMEs.: An exploratory survey among SMEs in the mechanical and electrical engineering sector in The Netherlands. *Technovation, 22*(1), 1-13.

Kim, L. (1998). Crisis construction and organizational learning: Capability building in catching-up at Hyundai Motor. *Organization science*, *9*(4), 506-521.

Kogut, B., & Zander, U. (1992). Knowledge of the firm, combinative capabilities, and the replication of technology. *Organization science*, *3*(3), 383-397.

Kotabe, M., Srinivasan, S. S., &Aulakh, P. S. (2002).Multinationality and firm performance: The moderating role of R&D and marketing capabilities. *Journal of international business studies*, 79-97.

Krasnikov, A., &Jayachandran, S. (2008). The relative impact of marketing, research-and-development, and operations capabilities on firm performance.*Journal of Marketing*, *72*(4), 1-11.

Krikorian, A. D., & Steward, F. C. (2012). Biochemical differentiation: The biosynthetic potentialities of growing and quiescent tissue. *Plant physiology—a treatise, Steward, FC, ed*, *5*, 227-326.

Krishnan, H. A., & Park, D. (1998). Effects of top management team change on performance in downsized US companies. *MIR: Management International Review*, 303-319.

Lall, S. (1992). Technological capabilities and industrialization. *World development*, *20*(2), 165-186.

Lambe, C. J., Spekman, R. E., & Hunt, S. D. (2002). Alliance competence, resources, and alliance success: conceptualization, measurement, and initial test. *Journal of the academy of Marketing Science*, *30*(2), 141-158.

Lazaric, N., & Marengo, L. (2000). Towards a characterization of assets and knowledge created in technological agreements: some evidence from the automobile robotics sector. *Industrial and Corporate Change*, *9*(1), 53-86.

Leonard-Barton, D. (1992). Core capabilities and core rigidities: a paradox in managing new product development. Strategic management journal, 13(S1), 111-125.

Levinthal, D. A., & March, J. G. (1993). The myopia of learning. *Strategic management journal*, *14*(S2), 95-112.

Loo, S. (1982). Perspective on the application of plant cell and tissue culture. In Plant tissue culture 1982, ed. A. Fujiwara, pp. 19-24. Tokyo: Japanese Association for Plant Tissue Culture.

Lovell, C. K. (1993). Production frontiers and productive efficiency. *The measurement of productive efficiency: techniques and applications*, 3-67.

Lu, F., Song, G., Tang, J., Zhao, H., & Liu, L. (2008). Profitability of China's industrial firms (1978–2006). *China Economic Journal*, *1*(1), 1-31.

Lundvall, B. Å. (Ed.). (2010). *National systems of innovation: Toward a theory of innovation and interactive learning* (Vol. 2). Anthem Press.

Luo, Y. (2001). Dynamic capabilities in international expansion. *Journal of World Business*, *35*(4), 355-378.

Luo, Y. (2007). The independent and interactive roles of procedural, distributive, and interactional justice in strategic alliances. *Academy of Management Journal*, *50*(3), 644-664.

Mahoney, T. A., Jerdee, T. H., & Nash, A. N. (1960). Predicting managerial effectiveness. *Personnel Psychology*, *13*(2), 147-163.

Mani, S. (2005). Innovation capability in India's telecommunications equipment industry. *ICTs and Indian Economic Development, Economy, Work, Regulation*, 265-325.

Mariadoss, B. J., Tansuhaj, P. S., &Mouri, N. (2011). Marketing capabilities and innovation-based strategies for environmental sustainability: An exploratory investigation of B2B firms. *Industrial Marketing Management*, *40*(8), 1305-1318.

McElroy, J. C., Morrow, P. C., & Rude, S. N. (2001). Turnover and organizational performance: a comparative analysis of the effects of voluntary, involuntary, and reduction-in-force turnover. *Journal of Applied Psychology*,*86*(6), 1294.

Menrad, K. (2004). Innovations in the food industry in Germany. *Research Policy, 33*(6), 845-878.

Mentzer, M. S. (1996). Corporate downsizing and profitability in Canada.*Canadian Journal of Administrative Sciences/Revue Canadienne des Sciences de l'Administration, 13*(3), 237-250.

Miner, J. B. (1960). The effect of a course in psychology on the attitudes of research and development supervisors. *Journal of Applied Psychology, 44*(3), 224.

Misawa, M. (1977). Production of natural substances by plant cell cultures described in Japanese patents. In *Plant Tissue Culture and Its Bio-technological Application* (pp. 17-26). Springer Berlin Heidelberg

Mishra, A. K., & Mishra, K. E. (1994).The role of mutual trust in effective downsizing strategies. *Human Resource Management, 33*(2), 261-279.

Morel, G. (1965). Clonal propagation of orchids by meristem culture. *Cymbidium Soc News, 20*(3).

Morgan, N. A., Vorhies, D. W., & Mason, C. H. (2009).Market orientation, marketing capabilities, and firm performance. *Strategic Management Journal,30*(8), 909-920.

Morris, J. R., Cascio, W. E., & Young, C. E. (2000). Downsizing after all these years: Questions and answers about who did it, how many did it, and who benefited from it. *Organizational Dynamics, 27*(3), 78-87.

Mueller, D. C., & Reardon, E. A. (1993). Rates of return on corporate investment. *Southern Economic Journal*, 430-453.

Murashige, T. (1977). Clonal crops through tissue culture. In *Plant tissue culture and its bio-technological application* (pp. 392-403). Springer Berlin Heidelberg.

Murashige, T. (1978). The impact of plant tissue culture on agriculture. *Frontiers of plant tissue culture, 15*, 26.

Nair, A., & Filer, L. (2003).Cointegration of firm strategies within groups: a long-run analysis of firm behavior in the Japanese steel industry. Strategic Management Journal, 24(2), 145-159.

Narula, R. (2004). R&D collaboration by SMEs: new opportunities and limitations in the face of globalisation. *Technovation, 24*(2), 153-161.

Nash, A. N. (1966). Development of an SVIB key for selecting managers.*Journal of applied psychology, 50*(3), 250.

Nelson, R. R., & Winter, S. G. (2009). *An evolutionary theory of economic change.* Harvard University Press.

Newey, L. R., & Zahra, S. A. (2009). The evolving firm: How dynamic and operating capabilities interact to enable entrepreneurship. *British Journal of Management, 20*(s1), S81-S100.

O'Connor, P. M., & Quinn, L. (2004).Organizational capacity for leadership.*The Center for Creative Leadership handbook of leadership development, 2*, 417-437.

OECD (2001), OECD Annual Report 2001, OECD Publishing, Paris.DOI: http://dx.doi.org/10.1787/annrep-2001-en

Ogawa, K., & Kitasaka, S. I. (1999). Market valuation and the q theory of investment. *Japanese Economic Review, 50*(2), 191-211.

O'Regan, N., & Ghobadian, A. (2004). Leadership and strategy: Making it happen. *Journal of General Management, 29*(4), 76-92.

Papadopoulos, I., & Karagouni, G. (2007, March). European timber trade analysis: an economical overview and regional market potential. In *International Workshop, Larnaka–Cyprus* (pp. 22-23).

Parida, V. (2008). Small firm capabilities for competitiveness an empirical study of ICT related small Swedish firms.

Parida, V., Pemartín, M., &Frishammar, J. (2009). The impact of networking practices on small firm innovativeness and performance: a multivariate approach. *International Journal of Technoentrepreneurship, 2*(2), 115-133.

Pasternack, B. A., Williams, T. D., & Anderson, P. F. (2001). Beyond the cult of the CEO: Building institutional leadership. *Strategy and Business*, 68-81.

Pearce, C. L., & Conger, J. A. (2003).All those years ago. *Shared leadership: Reframing the hows and whys of leadership*, 1-18.

Penrose, E. T. (1959). The Theory of the Growth of the Firm. New York: John Wiley & Sons.

Perdomo-Ortiz, J., González-Benito, J., &Galende, J. (2006). Total quality management as a forerunner of business innovation capability. *Technovation,26*(10), 1170-1185.

Peteraf, M. A. (1993). The cornerstones of competitive advantage: a resource-based view. Strategic management journal, 14(3), 179-191.

Porter, M. E. (1990). The competitive advantage of nations. *Harvard business review*.

Porter, M. E. (2000). Location, competition, and economic development: Local clusters in a global economy. *Economic development quarterly*, *14*(1), 15-34.

Porter, M. E. (2004). Building the microeconomic foundations of prosperity: Findings from the business competitiveness index. *World Competitiveness Report, 2005*.

Porter, M. E., & Millar, V. E. (1985). How information gives you competitive advantage.

Poulis, E., & Jackson, P. (2007, September).Dynamic capabilities in dynamic landscapes.In *British Academy of Management (BAM) conference (Warwick), CD Proceedings edited by C. Saunders* (pp. 11-13).

Prahalad, C. K., & Hamel, G. (1990).The core competence of the corporation.*Boston (Ma), 1990*, 235-256.

Prakash, J. (1999, August). Factors influencing the development of the micropropagation industry: the experience in India. In *International Symposium on Methods and Markers for Quality Assurance in Micropropagation 530* (pp. 165-172).

Prakash, J. 2006. Micropropagation Industry In India: Biology And Business. Acta Hort. (ISHS) 725:293-300 http://www.actahort.org/books/725/725_36.htm

Prieto, I. M., Revilla, E., & Rodríguez-Prado, B. (2009). Building dynamic capabilities in product development: How do contextual antecedents matter?.*Scandinavian Journal of Management*, *25*(3), 313-326.

PUROHIT, S. D. (2013). *Introduction to plant cell tissue and organ culture*. PHI Learning Pvt. Ltd..

Rappaport, A., Bancroft, E., &Okum, L. (2003). The aging workforce raises new talent management issues for employers. *Journal of Organizational Excellence*, *23*(1), 55-66.

Raymond, L., & St-Pierre, J. (2010). R&D as a determinant of innovation in manufacturing SMEs: An attempt at empirical clarification. *Technovation,30*(1), 48-56.

Rechinger C. 1893. Untersuchungen ¨uber die grenzen der Teilbarkeit in Pflanzenreich. *AbhandlungenzoologischbotanischenGessellschaft in Wien* 43: 310–334.

Reichstein, T., & Salter, A. (2006).Investigating the sources of process innovation among UK manufacturing firms. *Industrial and Corporate Change,15*(4), 653-682.

Richardson, W. H. (1972). Bayesian-based iterative method of image restoration. *JOSA*, *62*(1), 55-59.

Ripollés, M., & Blesa, A. (2012). International new ventures as "small multinationals": The importance of marketing capabilities. *Journal of World Business*, *47*(2), 277-287.

Rogers, M. (2004).Networks, firm size and innovation. *Small business economics*, *22*(2), 141-153.

Roodt, G., &Kotze, K. (2005). Factors that affect the retention of managerial and specialist staff: An exploratory study of an employee commitment model.*SA Journal of Human Resource Management*, *3*(2), 48-55.

Rothwell, R. (1992). Successful industrial innovation: critical factors for the 1990s. *R&D Management, 22*(3), 221-240.

Rush, H., Bessant, J., &Hobday, M. (2007).Assessing the technological capabilities of firms: developing a policy tool. *R&D Management, 37*(3), 221-236.

Sacco, J. M., & Schmitt, N. (2005).A dynamic multilevel model of demographic diversity and misfit effects. *Journal of Applied Psychology, 90*(2), 203.

Sanuri Mohd Mokhtar, S. (2013). The effects of customer focus on new product performance. *Business Strategy Series, 14*(2/3), 67-71.

Sarkar, M. B., Echambadi, R., Cavusgil, S. T., &Aulakh, P. S. (2001).The influence of complementarity, compatibility, and relationship capital on alliance performance. *Journal of the academy of marketing science, 29*(4), 358-373.

Sawyerr, O. O., McGee, J., & Peterson, M. (2003). Perceived Uncertainty and Firm Performance in SMEs The Role of Personal Networking Activities.*International Small Business Journal, 21*(3), 269-290.

Schendel, D. (1994). Introduction to the summer 1994 special issue—'Strategy: Search for New Paradigms'. *Strategic Management Journal, 15*(S2), 1-4.

Schneider, B., GOLDSTIEIN, H. W., & Smith, D. B. (1995). The ASA framework: An update. *Personnel psychology, 48*(4), 747-773.

Schuler, R. S., & Jackson, S. E. (1987).Linking competitive strategies with human resource management practices. *The Academy of Management Executive (1987-1989)*, 207-219.

Selznick, P. (2011). *Leadership in administration: A sociological interpretation*. Quid Pro Books.

Sethi, R., Smith, D. C., & Park, C. W. (2001). Cross-functional product development teams, creativity, and the innovativeness of new consumer products. *Journal of Marketing Research, 38*(1), 73-85.

Shan, W., Walker, G., &Kogut, B. (1994).Interfirm cooperation and startup innovation in the biotechnology industry. *Strategic management journal, 15*(5), 387-394.

Shefer, D., &Frenkel, A. (2005). R&D, firm size and innovation: an empirical analysis. *Technovation, 25*(1), 25-32.

Sher, P. J., & Yang, P. Y. (2005). The effects of innovative capabilities and R&D clustering on firm performance: the evidence of Taiwan's semiconductor industry. *Technovation, 25*(1), 33-43.

Sitkin, S. B. (1992). Learning through failure-The strategy of small losses.*Research in organizational behavior, 14*, 231-266.

Skoog, F., &Tsui, C. (1948). Chemical control of growth and bud formation in tobacco stem segments and callus cultured in vitro. *American Journal of Botany*, 782-787.

Slater, S. F., &Narver, J. C. (2000). The positive effect of a market orientation on business profitability: a balanced replication. *Journal of business research,48*(1), 69-73.

Smith, J. B., & Barclay, D. W. (1997). The effects of organizational differences and trust on the effectiveness of selling partner relationships. *the Journal of Marketing*, 3-21.

Sookaneknun, S., &Ussahawanitchakit, P. (2012).Transformational leadership, organizational innovation capability, and firm performance of cosmetic businesses in thailand. *Journal of international business & economics, 12*(4).

Souitaris, V. (2002). Firm–specific competencies determining technological innovation: A survey in Greece. *R&D Management, 32*(1), 61-77.

Steward, F. C., &Caplin, S. M. (1951). A tissue culture from potato tuber: The synergistic action of 2, 4-D and of coconut milk. *Science, 113*(2940), 518-520.

Steward, F. C., &Caplin, S. M. (1952). Investigations on Growth and Metabolism of Plant Cells III. Evidence for Growth Inhibitors in Certain Mature Tissues. *Annals of Botany, 16*(4), 477-489.

Stock, G. N., Greis, N. P., & Fischer, W. A. (2002).Firm size and dynamic technological innovation. *Technovation, 22*(9), 537-549.
Stovel, M., &Bontis, N. (2002). Voluntary turnover: knowledge management-friend or foe?. *Journal of intellectual Capital, 3*(3), 303-322.
Suri Babu, G., Mohana Rao, T., Ahmed, S., & Gupta, K. S. (2008). Relationship between leadership capability and knowledge management: A measurement approach. *Journal of Information & Knowledge Management,7*(02), 83-92.
Szulanski, G. (1996). Exploring internal stickiness: Impediments to the transfer of best practice within the firm. *Strategic management journal, 17*(S2), 27-43.
Tamayo-Torres, I., Ruiz-Moreno, A., &Verdú, A. J. (2010).The moderating effect of innovative capacity on the relationship between real options and strategic flexibility. *Industrial Marketing Management, 39*(7), 1120-1127.
Teece, D. J. (2009). *Dynamic Capabilities and Strategic Management: Organizing for Innovation and Growth: Organizing for Innovation and Growth*. Oxford University Press.
TEECE, D. J., PISANO, G., & SHUEN, A. (1997). Dynamic capabilities and strategic management. *Strategic management Journal, 18*(7), 509-533.
Temtime, Z. T., &Pansiri, J. (2004). Small business critical success/failure factors in developing countries: some evidences from Botswana.
Teo, H. H., Wan, W., Wang, X. W., & Wei, K. K. (2003). Effects of absorptive capacity on organizational predisposition toward information systems. *ICIS 2003 Proceedings*, 11.
Theodosiou, M., Kehagias, J., &Katsikea, E. (2012). Strategic orientations, marketing capabilities and firm performance: An empirical investigation in the context of frontline managers in service organizations. *Industrial Marketing Management, 41*(7), 1058-1070.
Thomas, G. F., Hocevar, S. P., & Jansen, E. (2006). *A diagnostic approach to building collaborative capacity in an interagency context* (no. Nps-gsbpp-06-013). Naval postgraduate school monterey ca graduate school of business and public policy.
Thomke, S., &Kuemmerle, W. (2000, August). Strategic assets, interdependence and technological change: an empirical investigation in pharmaceutical drug discovery. In *Academy of Management Proceedings* (Vol. 2000, No. 1, pp. I1-I6).Academy of Management.
Thornhill, S. (2006).Knowledge, innovation and firm performance in high-and low-technology regimes. *Journal of Business Venturing, 21*(5), 687-703.
Tidd, J., &Trewhella, M. J. (1997).Organizational and technological antecedents for knowledge acquisition and learning. *R&D Management, 27*(4), 359-375.
Tobin, J. (1969). A general equilibrium approach to monetary theory. *Journal of money, credit and banking, 1*(1), 15-29.
Tsai, W. (2001). Knowledge transfer in intraorganizational networks: Effects of network position and absorptive capacity on business unit innovation and performance. *Academy of management journal, 44*(5), 996-1004.
Tyler, B. B. (2001). The complementarity of cooperative and technological competencies: a resource-based perspective. *Journal of Engineering and technology management, 18*(1), 1-27.
Utterback, J. M. (1971). The process of technological innovation within the firm.*Academy of management Journal, 14*(1), 75-88.
Utterback, J. M., & Suarez, F. F. (1993).Innovation, competition, and industry structure. *Research policy, 22*(1), 1-21.
Van Overbeek, J., Conklin, M. E., & Blakeslee, A. F. (1941). Factors in coconut milk essential for growth and development of very young Daturaembryos.*Science, 94*(2441), 350-351.

Vance, C., & Larson, E. (2002).Leadership research in business and health care. *Journal of Nursing Scholarship*, *34*(2), 165-171.

Vasil, V., & Hildebrandt, A. C. (1965). Differentiation of tobacco plants from single, isolated cells in microcultures. *Science*, *150*(3698), 889-892.

Vertinsky, I. (2003). How can small firms compete successfully? Relative position, the choice of innovation strategies and innovation performance.*Frontiers of Entrepreneurship Research*.

Veugelers, R. (1997). Internal R & D expenditures and external technology sourcing. *Research policy*, *26*(3), 303-315.

Vieregger, C. H. (2013). *Three Essays on Strategic Capital Allocation* (Doctoral dissertation, washington university in st. Louis).

Vorhies, D. W. (1998). An investigation of the factors leading to the development of marketing capabilities and organizational effectiveness. *Journal of strategic marketing*, *6*(1), 3-23.

Wan, D., Ong, C. H., & Lee, F. (2005). Determinants of firm innovation in Singapore. *Technovation*, *25*(3), 261-268.

Wang, C. H., Lu, I. Y., & Chen, C. B. (2008).Evaluating firm technological innovation capability under uncertainty. *Technovation*, *28*(6), 349-363.

Wang, C. L., & Ahmed, P. K. (2007). Dynamic capabilities: A review and research agenda. *International journal of management reviews*, *9*(1), 31-51.

Weber, E. P., Lovrich, N. P., & Gaffney, M. J. (2007). Assessing collaborative capacity in a multidimensional world. *Administration & Society*, *39*(2), 194-220.

Went, F. W., &Thimann, K. V. (1937). Phytohormones. *Phytohormones*.

Wernerfelt, B. (1984). A resource-based view of the firm. Strategic management journal, *5*(2), 171-180.

White, P. R. (1954). The cultivation of animal and plant cells. *Soil Science*,*78*(1), 77.

White, P. R., & Braun, A. C. (1942). A cancerous neoplasm of plants. Autonomous bacteria-free crown-gall tissue. *Cancer Research*, *2*(9), 597-617.

Winter, S. G. (2003).Understanding dynamic capabilities. *Strategic management journal*, *24*(10), 991-995.

Woiceshyn, J., &Daellenbach, U. (2005). Integrative capability and technology adoption: evidence from oil firms. *Industrial and Corporate Change*, *14*(2), 307-342.

Wolfe, R. A. (1994). Organizational innovation: Review, critique and suggested research directions. *Journal of management studies*, *31*(3), 405-431.

Wong, V., Shaw, V., & Sher, P. J. (1999). Intra-firm learning in technology transfer: a study of Taiwanese information technology firms. *International Journal of Innovation Management*, *3*(04), 427-458.

Working Group Report. (2007). Horticulture, Plantation Crops and Organic Farming. In XI Five Year Plan (2002-2007). Pp-215.

Wu, J. (2013). Marketing capabilities, institutional development, and the performance of emerging market firms: A multinational study. *International Journal of Research in Marketing*, *30*(1), 36-45.

Xie, W., & White, S. (2004). Sequential learning in a Chinese spin-off: the case of Lenovo Group Limited. R&D Management, 34(4), 407-422.

Yam, R. C., Guan, J. C., Pun, K. F., & Tang, E. P. (2004). An audit of technological innovation capabilities in Chinese firms: some empirical findings in Beijing, China. *Research policy*, *33*(8), 1123-1140.

Yam, R. C., Lo, W., Tang, E. P., & Lau, A. K. (2011). Analysis of sources of innovation, technological innovation capabilities, and performance: An empirical study of Hong Kong manufacturing industries. *Research Policy*, *40*(3), 391-402.

Yamin, S., &Mavondo, F. T. (2015, January). Organizational Innovation: Relationship with Functional Strategies and Organizational Performance. In*Proceedings of the 2000 Academy of Marketing Science (AMS) Annual Conference* (pp. 296-301). Springer International Publishing.

Yu, G. C., & Park, J. S. (2006).The effect of downsizing on the financial performance and employee productivity of Korean firms. *International Journal of Manpower, 27*(3), 230-250.

Zahra, S. A., & George, G. (2002). Absorptive capacity: A review, reconceptualization, and extension. *Academy of management review, 27*(2), 185-203.

Zahra, S. A., Ireland, R. D., &Hitt, M. A. (2000). International expansion by new venture firms: International diversity, mode of market entry, technological learning, and performance. *Academy of Management journal, 43*(5), 925-950.

Zahra, S. A., Sapienza, H. J., &Davidsson, P. (2006). Entrepreneurship and dynamic capabilities: a review, model and research agenda. *Journal of Management studies, 43*(4), 917-955.

Zelbst, P. J., Green Jr, K. W., Abshire, R. D., & Sower, V. E. (2010). Relationships among market orientation, JIT, TQM, and agility. *Industrial Management & Data Systems, 110*(5), 637-658.

Zenk, M. H. (1978). The impact of plant cell culture on industry. *Frontiers of plant tissue culture, 1978*, 1-13.

Zhou, K. Z., & Wu, F. (2010). Technological capability, strategic flexibility, and product innovation. *Strategic Management Journal, 31*(5), 547-561.

Zollo, M., &Winter, S. G. (2002a). Deliberate learning and the evolution of dynamic capabilities. *Organization science, 13*(3), 339-351.

Zollo, M., Reuer, J. J., & Singh, H. (2002b).Interorganizational routines and performance in strategic alliances. *Organization Science, 13*(6), 701-713.

www.ingramcontent.com/pod-product-compliance
Lightning Source LLC
Chambersburg PA
CBHW061440180526
45170CB00004B/1500